# Practicing Greatness

# Practicing Greatness

## 7 Disciplines of Extraordinary Spiritual Leaders

Reggie McNeal

Foreword by Ken Blanchard

A LEADERSHIP ❖ NETWORK PUBLICATION

JOSSEY-BASS
A Wiley Imprint
www.josseybass.com

Published by Jossey-Bass
A Wiley Imprint
989 Market Street, San Francisco, CA 94103-1741   www.josseybass.com

Jossey-Bass books and products are available through most bookstores. To contact Jossey-Bass
directly, call our Customer Care Department within the U.S. at 800-956-7739, outside the
U.S. at 317-572-3986, or fax 317-572-4002.

Jossey-Bass also publishes its books in a variety of electronic formats. Some content that
appears in print may not be available in electronic books.

**Library of Congress Cataloging-in-Publication Data**

McNeal, Reggie.
    Practicing greatness : 7 disciplines of extraordinary spiritual leaders / Reggie McNeal ;
foreword by Ken Blanchard.— 1st ed.
        p. cm.
    Includes bibliographical references and index.
    ISBN-13: 978-0-7879-7753-5 (cloth)
    ISBN-10: 0-7879-7753-5 (cloth)
    1. Christian leadership. 2. Leadership—Religious aspects—Christianity. I. Title.
BV652.1.M42 2006
253—dc22                                                              2006000530

Printed in the United States of America
FIRST EDITION
*HB Printing*     10 9 8 7 6 5 4 3

# Leadership Network Titles

*The Millennium Matrix: Reclaiming the Past, Reframing the Future of the Church*, by M. Rex Miller

*Shaped by God's Heart: The Passion and Practices of Missional Churches*, by Milfred Minatrea

*The Ascent of a Leader: How Ordinary Relationships Develop Extraordinary Character and Influence*, by Bill Thrall, Bruce McNicol, and Ken McElrath

*The Missional Leader: Equipping Your Church to Reach a Changing World*, by Alan J. Roxburgh and Fred Romanuk

*The Elephant in the Boardroom: Speaking the Unspoken About Pastoral Transitions*, by Carolyn Weese and J. Russell Crabtree

# Contents

*To all great spiritual leaders—*
*we have been blessed by you*

# About Leadership Network

Since 1984, Leadership Network has fostered church innovation and growth by diligently pursuing its far-reaching mission statement: *To identify, connect, and help high-capacity Christian leaders multiply their impact.*

While Leadership Network's techniques adapt and change as the Church faces new opportunities and challenges, the organization's work follows a consistent and proven pattern: Leadership Network brings together entrepreneurial leaders who are focused on similar ministry initiatives. The ensuing collaboration—often across denominational lines—provides a strong base from which individual leaders can better analyze and refine their individual strategies. Peer-to-peer interaction, dialogue, and sharing inevitably accelerate participants' own innovations and ideas. Leadership Network further enhances this process through the development and distribution of highly targeted ministry tools and resources—including audio and video programs, special reports, e-publications, and online downloads.

With Leadership Network's assistance, today's Christian leaders are energized, equipped, inspired, and better able to multiply their own dynamic Kingdom-building initiatives.

Launched in 1996 in conjunction with Jossey-Bass, a Wiley Imprint, Leadership Network Publications present thoroughly researched and innovative concepts from leading thinkers, practitioners, and pioneering churches. The series collectively draws from a wide range of disciplines with individual titles providing perspective on one or more of five primary areas:

- Enabling effective leadership
- Encouraging life-changing service
- Building authentic community
- Creating Kingdom-centered impact
- Engaging cultural and demographic realities

For additional information on the mission or activities of Leadership Network, please contact:

Leadership Network
www.leadnet.org
(800) 765-5323
client.care@leadnet.org

# Foreword

When Reggie McNeal asked me if I would be willing to write a foreword for his book *Practicing Greatness*, it took me only a nanosecond to say yes, because Reggie is talking about a different kind of greatness. The greatness he is talking about is not a position or a destination, but a quality of leadership that blesses other people. Hallelujah! As Reggie points out, while bad leadership is to be avoided and good leadership helps us get things done, we need great leadership to raise the level of blessing for the human race. That is so consistent with my journey to truth about leadership.

In the late 1980s, when I turned my life over to the Lord and began to read the Bible, I realized that everything I ever wrote—everything I ever taught—Jesus did, and he did it perfectly, beyond my ability to describe or portray. And he did it with twelve inexperienced, unknowledgeable characters. His leadership was so effective that this ragtag group was able to carry on his vision and mission in such a way that it still impacts the world today. Jesus challenged us all to serve, rather than to be served as leaders. His leadership blessed people, and that should be the model for spiritual leaders. Yet sadly, often it is not. That's why I think *Practicing Greatness* is a must read for all people who want to lead at a higher level.

In *Practicing Greatness*, Reggie contends that spiritual leaders self-select into greatness by practicing seven lifelong disciplines: self-awareness, self-development, self-management, missional clarity, making good decisions, engaging with people, and cultivating aloneness. He devotes a chapter to each of these disciplines, identifying the strategic issues in each that can help leaders practice what is most important to do as the leader. This is why I think *Practicing Greatness* is a hard-hitting leadership book, not just a collection of inspirational thoughts.

If you want to make a difference in the lives of the people you touch, read *Practicing Greatness* and begin the journey. While Reggie devotes a fair amount of time to self—self-awareness and self-management—he definitely believes that leadership is not about you. Although it starts on the inside, it moves to the outside when you realize that greatness begins with a clear vision that inspires people to get into the act of forgetting about themselves and committing to the greatest good.

Thanks, Reggie. *Practicing Greatness* will make a difference.

Ken Blanchard, coauthor of *The One Minute Manager*®
and *Lead Like Jesus*
San Diego, California
March 2006

# Acknowledgments

I am privileged to routinely intersect with the lives of many extraordinary spiritual leaders and to learn from them. They have provided the insights for this volume. Many of them afford me close-hand observation of greatness-in-process. My editor, Sheryl Fullerton, has practiced her craft expertly in maintaining balance between "you can do it," "are you sure you want to do this?" and "let's get it done!" Lee Douglas, my assistant, does an amazing job in managing many aspects of my world so I can carve out writing time. As always, Cathy (my wife) provides me with phenomenal emotional and spiritual encouragement. Cate, you are the greatest!

# Practicing Greatness

# INTRODUCTION
## Needed: Great Spiritual Leaders

"Deliberate mediocrity is a sin." I can still recall the moment I heard Elton Trueblood speak those opening words in chapel at the seminary I attended over three decades ago. I honestly don't remember anything else he said because I was so stunned by that first sentence. Despite his quiet Quaker spirit and diminutive presence, Trueblood roared a challenge that caused my spirit immediately to leap, as if suddenly shot with adrenaline. Years later I am still as thrilled and motivated by them as when I first heard them. They were—and still are—words of liberation for me.

### Characteristics of Greatness

Up until that morning I had bought into the prevailing notion that aspiring to greatness was somehow unbecoming to a Christian. I had grown up in a spiritual culture that viewed the desire to be great as pitted against the virtue of humility.

### Humility

Since then I have learned that greatness in the kingdom of God is a journey toward humility. I also now understand that humility does not correlate with low spotlight. Plenty of no-names are racked by envy, jealousy, and pride. Being obscure does not render a leader humble. Nor does being famous automatically rule out being humble. Humility and celebrity can coexist. Jesus proves this point. Humility derives from the leader's awareness of where his or her source of strength lies. The ambition to become a great spiritual leader actually frees the spirit from the idolatry of self-centeredness, because greatness in the spiritual world cannot be pursued without cultivating God-consciousness.

The difficulty with which some spiritual leaders acknowledge their ambition to seek greatness betrays its motivation. They are looking for greatness that is found in position and power. Jesus dealt with this mutant strain of ambition in two close-occurring episodes with his initial band of disciples. Mark (9:33–35, NIV) tells the story:

> They came to Capernaum. When he was in the house, he asked them, "What were you arguing about on the road?" But they kept quiet because on the way they had argued about who was the greatest. Sitting down, Jesus called the Twelve and said, "If anyone wants to be first, he must be the very last, and the servant of all."

Apparently, the disciples didn't get it. Before long the group was again racked by dissension caused by their worldly ambition (Mark 10:35–45, NIV):

> Then James and John, the sons of Zebedee, came to him.
> "Teacher," they said, "we want you to do for us whatever we ask."
>
> "What do you want me to do for you?" he asked.
>
> They replied, "Let one of us sit at your right and the other at your left in your glory."
>
> "You don't know what you are asking," Jesus said. "Can you drink the cup I drink or be baptized with the baptism I am baptized with?"
>
> "We can," they answered. Jesus said to them, "You will drink the cup I drink and be baptized with the baptism I am baptized with, but to sit at my right or left is not for me to grant. These places belong to those for whom they have been prepared."
>
> When the ten heard about this, they became indignant with James and John. Jesus called them together and said, "You know that those who are regarded as rulers of the Gentiles lord it over them, and their high officials exercise authority over them. Not so with

you. Instead, whoever wants to become great among you must be your servant, and whoever wants to be first must be slave of all. For even the Son of Man did not come to be served, but to serve, and to give his life as a ransom for many."

In neither discussion does Jesus disparage the ambition to be great. Nor does he float the idea of greatness as something his follower-leaders might aspire to. Rather, he takes it for granted that their motivations would push them toward achieving greatness. He just wants to point them in the right direction. He seizes the moment to contrast the prevailing notions of greatness with the genuine article and to challenge them to see greatness in spiritual terms. Jesus' idea of greatness revolves around humility and service—a far cry from our typical associations with this concept.

Jesus' disciples often still don't get it when it comes to the pursuit of greatness. Unfortunately, plenty of people who posture themselves as spiritual leaders hunger for the worldly trappings of greatness: position, power, and privilege. Many leaders in the church industry evidence the same ambitions as business executives or politicians. Calling this ambition something else ("call" or "mission" or any number of other euphemisms that spiritual leaders frequently invoke) doesn't make it any less what it really is. Unfortunately, the current culture of the North American church seems to reward this lack of character rather than to repudiate it. No wonder our witness to the world is stunted! People see through such pretensions.

## Effectiveness

Greatness is not just about character. It's also about effectiveness. When Jesus talked about serving others as part of his definition of greatness, he assumed that the service would actually be helpful to its recipients and that the leaders would be accomplished. Jesus was not incompetent, nor did he look for that quality in others. He did not choose the twelve apostles based on their lack of ability. After all, he was going to trust the movement to them. Paul was never asked to give up his critical thinking or lay aside his determination (both are attributes of great leaders). In fact all great leaders in the Bible are characterized by their effectiveness, as well as character. They didn't just have great hearts; they had great capacity to deliver.

## Willingness to Serve

As for service as a quality of leadership greatness, we typically think of service in terms of acts of helping, supporting, encouraging, being kind—these sorts of expressions. This is too restrictive. Servant leadership is an attitude, not a genre of narrowly circumscribed actions. Service is about a desired outcome, not just the type of action a leader takes on behalf of others. Jesus served the rich young ruler when he challenged his value system. He served the woman at the well when he probed her pattern of broken relationships. He even served the Pharisees when chasing them out of the Temple. In every case those Jesus served made choices of their own in their responses, but that did not negate his acts of service to them.

Great leaders bless people. They inspire and encourage. They help people become more than what they have been, maybe even more than they thought they could be. Great leaders help people be a part of something bigger than themselves. In short, great leaders leave people better off than they were before the leader entered their lives.

## Need for Great Leaders

Unfortunately, this is not what many of us experience. Bad leaders are a form of evil. They curse people by diminishing their life. They rob people of hope. They reduce people's dreams and expectations for their lives. They discourage and disparage people. They leave people worse off than when they found them. Bad leadership is not always the result of bad character or intentional malevolence. It can result from simple incompetence.

Good leaders are usually adequate to the leadership demands placed on them. Good leaders get things done. They keep things going. They assess situations and devise solutions. They organize people to accomplish tasks and help people in the process. Good leaders are shorter in supply than they should be. We could use many more good leaders, as anyone who has suffered under bad leadership will attest. In normal times, we can generally get by with good leaders.

But we do not live in normal times. You may have noticed that we are in a vortex of transitional forces that are creating a new world. We need *great* leaders to help us get through the wormhole of overlapping universes of premoderns, moderns, and postmoderns—all sharing the same space on this planet. We need great leaders who will display both courage and wisdom in the face of unprecedented challenges in bioethics, global terrorism, economic realignments, and the information revolution, to name a few.

We are desperate for great leaders in every sector of our society—in politics, the social sector, health care, education, the arts, sports, and community agencies, as well as at local, regional, and national levels. We need leaders who distinguish themselves as great, mostly by the positive impact they have on the people they lead.

We are even more desperate for great *spiritual* leaders. The postmodern world is wildly spiritual, in contrast to the modern world of the last five centuries, which has seemed intent on draining mystery from life and the universe. Postmoderns realize that life is more than physical and financial and technological and functional. They are in a determined search for meaning and significance (contrary to predictions not many years ago that nihilism would be the philosophical choice for successors to modernity). This widespread yearning begs for spiritual leadership.

Postmoderns do not link their search for spirituality to the church, or if they do, they don't limit their options in spirituality to organized religion. People take their life issues to the office, to school, and to the club, not just to the counselor's office or Sunday School class. This reality means we need spiritual leaders in all avenues of life and culture. We need business leaders, educators, health sector leaders, scientists, and information specialists who are great in their spiritual capacities. Acknowledging and expanding our notion of spiritual leadership to the "pedestrian" arenas of life does not diminish the continued need for them. Our understanding of the sphere of spiritual leadership must include the busy street as well as the quiet cloister. While the suggestions for practicing greatness contained in this book may have primary application for those who are designated practitioners of spiritual leadership, the insights hold true for leaders across the board.

Leaders who have an appropriate view of self (humility), combined with the capacity to help others (service), don't just show up in the nick of time. They are crafted over time. They practice being great. Extraordinary character and exceptional competence develop over time. Leaders must make countless good choices and right calls to fashion greatness.

Practicing greatness requires that the spiritual leader develop some key "disciplines." These are self-awareness, self-management, self-development, mission, decision making, belonging, and aloneness. Some might not consider these as disciplines in a classic sense. However, great spiritual leaders habitually practice each of these disciplines just as surely as Olympic athletes commit themselves to a physical regimen or concert violinists dedicate themselves to running scales. Other leaders may visit one or more of these practices, intentionally or unintentionally. Great spiritual leaders are committed, consciously and intentionally, to all seven of them.

1. *The discipline of self-awareness* is most important because it protects leaders from being self-absorbed or merely role-driven. Leaders do not arrive at self-awareness all at once. Life experience adds to this integration of mission, talent, and personality.

2. *The discipline of self-management* acknowledges that great leaders are great managers, not just of others but, primarily and foremost, of themselves. Failure to manage oneself leaves a leader vulnerable to self-sabotage or derailment.

3. *The discipline of self-development* characterizes all great leaders. They never stop growing. Leaders who adopt this discipline as a life habit pursue lifelong learning and build on their strengths. They also choose to grow through failure.

4. *The discipline of mission* honors the propensity of great leaders to give themselves to great causes. They order their lives missionally. They have decided how to spend their lives focused on their mission rather than allow their lives to be hijacked by others' expectations and agendas or dissipated by distractions that debilitate their energies.

5. *The discipline of decision making* sets great leaders apart from good run-of-the-mill leaders. Great leaders consistently make good decisions. They know how to make decisions, when to make decisions, and what decisions need to be made.

6. *The discipline of belonging* characterizes great leaders' ability to enjoy significant relationships that nurture their lives. They not only value and practice community but also make a conscious decision to belong to others. They belong despite the risk, because they know that to quit risking is to quit loving and that to quit loving is to quit leading in the spiritual arena.

7. *The discipline of aloneness* celebrates great leaders' capacity not only to endure the loneliness of leadership but to actually build solitude into their lives. They appreciate the depth of soul making that is possible only in solitude and in heart-to-heart exchanges with their Leader.

## The Intent of This Book

This book is not intended as a put-down to good leaders. We need good leaders, especially if the alternative is more poor leaders. *But we are desperate for great leaders*. This book aims to encourage many of you to choose a path toward greatness. Perhaps you are already on the journey. I am writing to help you stay the course. Or maybe you have contemplated the journey but are unsure of its requirements. This volume helps you know what is in store if you start up this trail. If you have wondered whether merely the yearning for this adventure is itself somehow inappropriate and self-promoting, you will discover that the way of spiritual greatness is the way of escape from lesser passions that define most leaders and constrict their influence. If you're someone who just needs to be liberated to pursue greatness—to give you permission to escape self-imposed mediocrity—this book is also for you.

In the spiritual realm, greatness is not pursued for greatness' sake. Perhaps this statement should go without saying, but to do so would run an unwarranted risk of a colossal misunderstanding about the pursuit of greatness for spiritual leaders. Genuinely great spiritual leaders do not do what they do for themselves or even as a way to become recognized as great leaders. The end game for spiritual leaders is about expanding the kingdom of God. They pursue greatness because they are passionate about God and about helping other people experience the life God intended for them to enjoy. In the end, great spiritual leaders are not interested in calling attention to themselves. They point people to a great God. This is the sort of greatness we are desperate for.

Greatness is earned. It is not a gift; it is a reward. It is not accidental; it is cultivated. It is not bestowed by others; it is self-determined. You do not need to hope it happens. You can plot a course to make it happen. "Am I a great leader?" or "Do I want to be a great leader?" are questions only you can answer. You *will* answer them one way or another. The kingdom of God is at stake.

You are free to choose to practice greatness.

# 1

# THE DISCIPLINE OF
# SELF-AWARENESS

Harold didn't quite see it coming. The young pastor had enjoyed phenomenal and early success in the ministry. Every assignment he had attempted went well. His reputation for being an effective leader grew right along with the church he had planted. However, without Harold realizing it, the church crossed a threshold. It outgrew him.

Harold was unaware of some basic truths about himself, for example, his tendency to micromanage at the same time that he resisted accountability. The first problem drove his staff crazy and led to constant turnover that greatly reduced his congregation's capacity to sustain ministry momentum. The second shortcoming—his unwillingness to be accountable—eventually got him in hot water with the church's key leaders. When the church was small, Harold could make unilateral, on-the-fly decisions. But when the church numbered hundreds, with dozens of leaders involved and vested in their own ministries, Harold's decisions rippled out into unanticipated consequences. Eventually, his shortcomings caught up with Harold. Leaders and many in the congregation questioned his credibility and lost trust in him. Eventually, attendance and membership began to decline.

Harold was bewildered by this turn of events in his ministry. He knew it wasn't working anymore, but he didn't know why. Yet he plunged ahead, doing all the wrong things. In his frustration, Harold began making even more decisions on his own, adopted a more frenetic pace, and became more anxious and demanding—all of which alienated even more people who could have been great partners. His own fears about his ineffectiveness and what was going on in the church translated into a refusal to receive feedback, which drove him into a corner and accelerated his demise as a leader. Harold was suffering from a lack of self-awareness. And the costs of that deficit bankrupted his leadership.

Jim closed the door to his office, just as he did every day, but not so he could concentrate, or study, or pray. He closed the door so he could sleep. He slept for hours every day, but he never felt rested. Eventually, Jim recognized that he was depressed. He contacted his internist for a physical, then for a referral to a counselor. He also engaged a spiritual director. After a few weeks, Jim made the courageous decision to secure a sabbatical from his elders so he could concentrate his energies on exploring some personal demons that were threatening to destroy him, his family, and his ministry. Jim took a very intentional journey of self-discovery.

Some months later, Jim returned to his leadership responsibilities armed with new insights into himself. He established new accountabilities and boundaries for his life that were designed to protect him from a relapse of his emotional exhaustion. He implemented a new team structure, demonstrating his decision to trust other people with the church's ministry. His leadership, now vastly improved, guided the church into renewal. Jim went from being a leader on the way down to a leader determined to be great. His increased self-awareness set the stage for this transition.

The single most important piece of information a leader possesses is self-awareness. The dictionary uses a variety of words to portray the meaning of awareness: *knowledge, mindful, vigilance, conscious, alert,* to note a few. When you add the word *self* to these, you get a good idea of what self-awareness includes: self-knowledge (knowing who you are), self-mindfulness (understanding your motives for doing what you do), self-vigilance (knowing what makes you tick and what ticks you off!), self-consciousness (knowing how you come across to others), and self-alertness (maintaining your emotional, physical, and spiritual condition). The discipline of self-awareness, then, is the leader's intentional quest for self-understanding.

The hazards for leaders of not being self-aware are serious and can even be deadly. Without this insight into themselves and their behavior and motivations, leaders become subject to unknown or underappreciated forces that influence their actions and that can sabotage their work. Without appropriate self-awareness, hidden addictions or compulsions may guide leaders to behaviors that create huge problems and may dismay, exasperate, and bewilder those they lead. Leaders who operate without self-awareness run the risk of being blindsided by destructive impulses and confused by emotions that threaten to derail their agenda and leadership effectiveness. They may overestimate or underestimate their abilities and respond unpredictably. For followers, credibility rides or falls on consistency—something leaders short on self-awareness usually do not have. In short, leaders lacking self-awareness are besieged from within. They often are their own worst enemy. And they don't even know it!

On the other hand, leaders who know themselves have gained their best ally—themselves! Self-awareness gifts them with significant insight. They know why they are on the planet and what contribution they intend to make—and they are in hot pursuit of making it. They know the behaviors and values that support their mission. They know how to measure their success. They know what they bring to the table in terms of talent and abilities. They know what they don't know, so they are constantly pushing their learning in strategic areas that support their personal growth and missional effectiveness.

Self-awareness touches all the other disciplines because it is foundational to every other element of greatness. Interestingly, it is also the capstone of the leader's journey. At the end of the road, great leaders are intimately acquainted with themselves. What's more, they are at home with themselves. This stands in sharp contrast to the legion of leaders who are attempting their assignment with nobody home.

## The Self-Awareness of Biblical Leaders

Leaders in the Bible frequently reflect a high degree of self-understanding.

### David

David demonstrates the power of self-awareness in establishing and protecting a personal sense of identity. He calls himself "the Lord's anointed." This phrase obviously called to mind the mysterious episode in David's childhood when Samuel, the prophet, showed up at his home and anointed him as the future king of Israel.

This phrase—the Lord's anointed—both captured and reflected a core understanding that David had of himself: he was the Lord's anointed, not just Samuel's. This meant he had a special relationship with God. One cannot read David's psalms without encountering this conviction. Psalm 23 details the care of the Shepherd-God for the shepherd-king. Psalm 139 rehearses the extraordinary connections between David and God, beginning in the womb and throughout his life (his thoughts, his words, his physical location—even his sleep!). The confessions of Psalm 51 reflect that David considered his relationship to God to be more important than his pride. It frightened him that his sin might rupture this special connection, so he pleaded for God's continued presence and restoration.

### Paul

Paul's autobiographical statements in Philippians 3 reveal how self-awareness can integrate key components of a leader's life. The apostle's sense of self was composed of his Jewish roots, his early training as a Pharisee, his passionate nature, and his hunger for significance. He admitted to the impact of his family of origin ("of the tribe of Benjamin, a Hebrew of Hebrews," v. 5). He acknowledged his early blindness to Christ ("in regard to the law, a Pharisee," v. 5). The apostle did this without disparaging the underlying heart hunger that drove him to devour the law. That unsatisfied appetite was finally satisfied in his relationship with Jesus.

Paul knew what he was after in life ("the prize for which God has called me heavenward in Christ Jesus," v. 14). He had obviously nurtured a personal vision of what Jesus had foreseen that he could be when the Lord captured him on the road to Damascus. Paul's sense of self was radically and forever altered in the dust, darkness, and light of that experience.

The persecutor-turned-missionary stamped the entire Christian movement with a missionary fervor. This zeal flowed directly out of Paul's understanding of God's merciful and relentless heart for him, even when he was God's enemy. We know a God of grace partly because Paul knew a gracious God. The converted Pharisee was willing to rethink his monocultural worldview. This dynamic enabled the movement to spread cross-culturally under Paul's leadership.

## Jesus

Even Jesus had to grow in self-awareness. He evidenced an emerging self-understanding in his Temple visit at age twelve. He seemed to be coming to grips with his unique relationship with his Father. We can only imagine what triggered Jesus' realization that he was profoundly different from all the other boys and girls. Surely, his parents' recitation of the events surrounding his birth contributed to his understanding. However, Jesus had to explore these insights for himself, as would any human child.

Perhaps his cousin John's outburst at his public baptism ("look, the lamb of God who takes away the sin of the world," John 1:26, NIV), coupled with the voice from heaven, were the moments when Jesus crystallized his ideas about who he was and the nature of his mission. In the wilderness temptations that immediately followed Jesus' baptism, Satan challenged key aspects of Jesus' personhood. He attacked Jesus' trust and dependence on his Father (by asking him to turn stones to bread), urged him to gain notoriety without service (by inviting him to leap from the Temple), and offered him power and glory that avoided suffering and sacrifice (if he would acknowledge Satan as earth's ruler). Each of these temptations targeted a critical aspect of Jesus' realization of the nature and cost of his messianic identity and mission.

Jesus' public ministry and passion provide many instances of his self-awareness. Two examples, one from his early ministry and one from the last days, reflect Jesus' profound self-understanding. Early on, Jesus quizzed his disciples about what people were saying about him. Then he quizzed them to see if they could get it right.

> "Simon Peter answered, 'You are the Christ, the son of the living God.' Jesus replied, 'Blessed are you, Simon son of Jonah, for this was not revealed to you by man, but by my Father in heaven'" (Matthew 16:16–17, NIV). At the end, Jesus' prayer in the Garden of Gethsemane reflected a full sense of who he was ("Glorify your Son that your Son may glorify you" [John 17:1]), where he had come from, and where he was going ("And now, Father, glorify me in your presence with the glory I had with you before the world began" [John 17:5, NIV]).

Any less self-knowledge would have made it impossible for Jesus to endure the spiritual and physical agony of the cross.

These three leaders—David, Paul, and Jesus—certainly qualify for inclusion on anyone's list of great leaders. The foundation for their life achievements was dug and poured in their self-awareness. That is still today how great leaders secure their leadership.

But how do leaders go about improving their self-awareness? They do some serious investigating.

## Digging into Who You Are

None of us can cultivate self-awareness without understanding how we've become who we are. Gaining insight into who we are and how we became ourselves requires some serious digging and inspection, much the way an archaeologist unearths the origins and arti-facts of ancient civilization by excavating long-buried ruins. Lead-ers who want to foster greater self-awareness likewise need to reveal and understand the sources of their own identities, particularly their family of origin and its legacy and the significant personal experi-ences that have marked and shaped them.

## Your Family of Origin

We learn our first life lessons in our family of origin, then we spend the rest of our lives either building on these lessons or trying to over-come them. We learn whether we are blessed or not well before we can speak. We learn whether we are safe or violated well before we can express the ideas of security and boundaries. These lessons, attitudes, and behaviors are so deeply imprinted on our psyches that it often takes years for us even to know they are there and what their content is; they just feel normal, whatever they are. They are the warp and woof of who we are.

For most people, the most intense years of exploring family-of-origin issues tend to be in the twenties and thirties, sometimes all the way through the mid-forties. During this period, leaders have to achieve enough independence and separation from their family of origin to gain perspective on where their journeys have taken them. Still, a learning leader never stops gaining and integrating insights from the past throughout life. It's never too late to begin this jour-ney for personal development and growth. The problem is that some spiritual leaders never book this trip.

Great leaders distinguish themselves by hitting the trail of self-exploration early and being unrelenting in searching for clues to their own formation. They are not afraid to push into uncharted territory, even when the road seems fraught with danger. They are determined not to let their past govern their present. Intriguingly, the only way they can free themselves from the past is to explore it fully. Otherwise, leaders are dragging stuff around in their suitcases that they didn't pack and may not even know is there.

Leaders who do not excavate the family-of-origin site may miss some key personal insights that carry huge implications for their relationship skills. Communication patterns, capacity for intimacy, conflict-resolution skills, view of authority—all enormously important behaviors and attitudes in determining how we relate and respond to others—are initially formed and informed in our earliest years. Since leadership is mostly about managing relationships, this self-understanding proves crucial to leaders' effectiveness. Without this understanding, leaders might not know what is pushing their hot buttons or jerking their chain, so they condemn themselves to react to unidentified forces rather than to be in control of themselves.

Billy frequently lashed out in anger when anyone criticized him. As a result he created lots of problems for himself in terms of broken relationships. Even people who were Billy's friends found it difficult to make suggestions, lest they be dropped from the list of people he could "trust." Consequently, the leadership culture around Billy could best be characterized as a revolving door, where people cycled in and out. The problem was, they left bleeding. Only in marital counseling did Billy come to understand why he experienced such anger when challenged or confronted. He learned that his anger was a secondary emotional response to the primal emotion of fear.

The therapist helped Billy unearth the hidden secret to his flash-hot responses. As a kid Billy's mistakes or shortcomings were ridiculed and punished, often including physical whippings. He had learned to be afraid when he failed. Now years removed from that setting, the slightest hint of failure triggered his fear. Since Billy felt threatened, he fought back with his anger. Billy's "dig" into his family of origin armed him with a new awareness that allowed him to choose his responses rather than let his reactions be triggered by forces he did not comprehend.

All leaders have family-of-origin issues unique to them, even for those who emerge from the same family. That's because each person in a family experiences it differently for lots of reasons. Families are dynamic systems. Children are born into different stages of the parents' lives. Siblings often grow up in different surroundings (houses, cities, and economic status). Each child has a unique relationship with every other person in the family. In my own family of origin the children are spaced over seventeen years. My oldest brother (fifteen years my senior) has told me that he regrets I did not know my parents when they were young. But I also missed setting up house in a one-room store building, with sheets serving as walls. That was his experience in the post-World War II family move back home to Gainesville, Georgia, from the shipyards of Wilmington, North Carolina.

Often we speak of family of origin only in negative terms, but our goal here is not to look for deficits alone but to look also for gifts. From our family of origin we may take gifts such as humor, love, strong self-reliance, or emotional intelligence, to name a few possibilities. And the intent is not to blame parents or other family members for our own shortcomings. Actually, the evaluation of the impact of our family of origin allows us to take responsibility for who we are and how we behave and feel. Once we can name our particular challenges, they are ours. A few common themes that we will mention here are usually worth investigating.

## Your Blessing—or Not

The awareness of being a blessed child combines several key elements of experience in our family of origin, including a sense of being unconditionally accepted for who we are and not for what we do, being loved in an unshakeable way, and feeling valued and worthwhile. A blessed child has parents who provide positive expectations and experiences of empowerment, trust, and confidence. Blessed children build their lives on a platform of love, belonging, and acceptance.

We all want to be a blessed child. Not all of us are. But that doesn't stop us from searching for blessedness. That search can take a variety of forms. If we don't come from a family where we felt blessed, we sometimes work hard to prove to others that we are worth something. Or as we desperately try to gain other people's approval, we hand over our lives to their expectations and demands.

> Sheri worked herself into exhaustion, but still didn't let up. She took on any assignment, just so she could gain a word of approval. She even took affirmation from others' noticing how overworked she was. A sensitive supervisor finally recognized this pattern and helped her come to grips with the understanding that she was still trying to please a mother she never could, who was now a resident in an Alzheimer's care unit and would never be able to bless Sheri.

Some of us who had parents who did not bless us may harbor and nurture anger against them and rebel against anyone in authority over us. Pastors with this experience in their families of origin may resent the authority of the board. Staff members might resist the authority of the senior minister in a congregation or leader of the organization (which often shows up in criticism that is designed to diminish the leader's position and influence). Many spiritual leaders have derailed over this issue alone.

> Jerry thought he knew more than anyone in authority over him. His criticisms grew increasingly public to the point that he lost his job for insubordination. He still thinks the boss was too incompetent to see his brilliance and that he, in fact, intimidated his boss. Jerry doesn't get it. He had been mentored early on in his career by a man renowned for conflicts with authority—all related to his own unfinished business with a father who failed to bless him. Jerry now has a pathology in his relationships with supervisors and with accountability that threatens to make him ineffective as a leader, no matter where he winds up.

None of this is to suggest that an unblessed child who becomes a leader cannot be great. Moses was not blessed, yet who could deny his claim to greatness? The issue for leaders revolves around the degree to which they have assessed these family dynamics, examining them for symptoms of trying to overcompensate in ways that contribute to unhealthy life patterns that can lead to failure.

## Your Hidden Addictions and Compulsions

Addictions or compulsions such as problems with drugs or alcohol, sex addictions, a lust for power, compulsive eating, adrenaline addiction, workaholism, approval craving, just to name a few common ones, often stem from family-of-origin backgrounds. We know that the "sins of the fathers" are visited on down the generational chain. Addictive environments spawn people prone to addiction, though the object of addiction may change.

Although many leaders may come to recognize that alcohol or drug abuse is a problem, legions of others are unaware they are using food or work to anesthetize their heart pain brought on through loneliness or their inability to experience intimacy though surrounded by admirers. Others have no idea that their need for approval drives them to physical, emotional, mental, and spiritual exhaustion. They are just dying (literally) to hear, "We don't know what we'd do without you!"

Leaders can often be blessed in their dysfunction by unhealthy people and systems. Spiritual organizations are notorious for blessing workaholism, for instance. Without self-awareness of the dynamics of addictions and compulsions in their lives, leaders are doomed to be driven by them in unhealthy ways. "Adrenaline addiction" is an especially poignant case in point. Some leaders don't know why they are unwilling to break their work rhythms, to take time off, even though they know their lives are way out of balance. They don't like the "blues" they feel when they are withdrawing from adrenaline, so they maintain or generate artificially high stress levels, just to make sure their body is still pumping adrenaline into their system. They will even manufacture a reason for their body to stay at high alert to avoid the discomfort of coming down.

Fred, a spiritual leader in his late twenties, seemed unaware of the compulsions that were driving his choices and ruining his health, as well as threatening his family. He worked constantly, afraid to establish or to maintain any limits on what he was willing to do. His frenetic pace had little to do with loving people; it mostly had to do with pleasing them. Fred was afraid that he would be criticized for not being available when they called. His constant anxiety triggered another subconscious compulsion: Fred viewed food as comfort and nurture. Sleep-deprived, overweight, and anxious, Fred fell into a daze of being out of touch with others, himself, his family, and God. All the while he kept up appearances at corporate functions and fulfilled his leadership duties. But underneath the activity and the "God chatter" was a lonely, scared, tired person.

Fred's wife finally intervened, persuading him to seek some counseling. A skillful life coach helped Fred understand the underlying causes for his out-of-control life, reframe his assumptions about appropriate expectations, and establish new limits and behaviors; the coach provided some ongoing accountability. The road to recovery was not without detours and reversals (as is often the case), but within six months Fred had lost weight, was getting adequate sleep each night, and enjoyed a day off with his family and several uninterrupted weeknights at home each week. As he emerged from his compulsions, the fog lifted and Fred's personality began to reemerge. This took courage on his part, the loving support of his wife, and some good direction from an outside-the-system life coach.

## Your Boundaries—or Lack of Them

Many spiritual leaders discover that they get into psychological, emotional, and spiritual distress because they have inappropriate boundaries. Boundaries are like fences. They let us know where we end and where the rest of the world picks up. Some leaders have left gates open; some have let the fence be knocked down, and others have never figured out where the fence goes.

Henry Cloud and Steve Townsend[1] have identified four problematic boundary types: compliants, avoidants, controllers, and nonresponsives. Each condition carries a set of potential pitfalls for spiritual leaders, especially if they are unaware of the boundary violation.

*Compliants.*   Compliants are people who allow others to violate their personal boundaries, mainly because they don't want to "hurt others' feelings"—a telltale phrase indicating how compliants inappropriately take on the responsibility of managing other people's emotions. Consequently, compliants have a tough time saying no to people, even when the request for time or attention is out of line or too demanding. Even though compliants may be screaming inside for relief from others' demands, they usually give in and then seethe because of their lost time and energy.

Compliant leaders frequently harbor resentment toward the very people they claim they want to serve and blame others for their distress instead of recognizing that their own internal flaw is causing the problem. Because they fear abandonment or rejection, compliants leave the gate open when it should be shut, then blame others for coming in.

> Chloe is the classic compliant. She can't say no, yet she whines incessantly about how others take advantage of her. On the outside she is the consummate servant, always attentive to people's needs. On the inside she is a cauldron of resentment waiting to spill over. Unless she gets a handle on this, she is headed for burnout and bitterness. She will blame others for it, but her burnout will be her own doing.

Many spiritual leaders wrestle with this boundary issue. After all, people go into the ministry to help other people. What they discover is that the needs are enormous and never-ending. If leaders have cracks in their own psychological foundation that they are looking for others to fill (high approval needs, for instance), they are particularly susceptible to compliance issues.

Treatment for compliants involves the twin remedy of awareness (here we are again!) and accountability. Compliants have to come out of denial and own the dysfunction as their own. They have to quit blaming others for their dilemma and realize it is their own needs and fears that are the problem. Since this issue didn't develop overnight, it won't go away overnight. Leaders who make themselves accountable to others often ask for help in creating space for themselves and in establishing new work rhythms that include scheduled time when the leader is unavailable to others.

*Avoidants.* Avoidants evidence another set of boundary problems. In effect, they shut the gates when they should let others in; these leaders withdraw under pressure. Early family-of-origin experiences may lie at the root of the avoidant reaction. They may have had some experience of psychological pain that taught them an unfortunate lesson: keep other people out. Avoidants are very hard to help because they keep people, even those who want to help them, at a distance. They keep people out in a number of ways: by verbal gate-shutting (cutting off conversation with a curt "I'm fine"), by creating emotional distance (keeping their guard up), and even by physically withdrawing (from keeping the door shut to being physically absent). Spiritual leaders with this boundary problem wind up lonely and isolated, lacking the emotional and psychological support they need in a leadership role that places huge emotional and psychological demands on them. As a result, some leaders who fail to recognize and address this boundary issue crater. Their burnout may be either explosive or implosive.

> Eugene grew up as an only child of aging parents. Doted on and coddled, he developed high expectations of how others should treat him. Yet he never learned to play with other kids and was emotionally distant from his parents (they used material things as a poor substitute for emotionally engaging their son). Eugene became a loner. But he was a very competent leader, so his ministry experience for almost two decades was very successful. As his

church grew, Eugene found the pressure getting to him. He withdrew more and more, eventually becoming an absentee leader. Those who saw what was happening tried to help. He not only refused their offers of assistance, he withdrew from anyone who had "found him out." When his board began to raise the issue of his absences, he refused to be accountable. He finally exploded in a board meeting and quit. The sad thing was, some of his best friends were on the board. Eugene further alienated the very people who were his best promise for help.

Leaders with this boundary issue are hard to help, because that's the problem—being hard to reach and to help is the issue. It takes particularly committed friends who are willing to be patient and persistent in breaching the leader's wall. Occasionally, in a time of failure, the leader is open to coaching. This window of opportunity should not be ignored by those who can provide emotional and spiritual support.

*Controllers.* Controllers are people who don't respect others' boundaries and, in some cases, don't even realize that boundaries exist. Controllers come in two varieties: aggressive and passive. Aggressive controllers bull their way in where they shouldn't and feel they have a right to be there. Spiritual leaders who invade others' privacy or who are abusive with their spiritual authority fall into this category. They tell people how to think and how to live, and they even see others' money as something they are entitled to. In extreme form these are cult leaders who manipulate and abuse their followers. Passive controllers achieve their goals indirectly through guilt and manipulation, deceiving their followers into doing their bidding while letting them think it is their own choice. They are experts at hooking people at their points of vulnerability.

Alan is a bully. He brings people on board his staff leadership team by wooing them with high salaries and promises of advancement. He then manages them through intimidation, reminding them what they owe him and how hard it would be for them to find another job as good-paying as this. Alan is hardly subtle in his controlling ways. He's the aggressive type.

Sandra, soft-spoken and sweet as honey, is never someone you'd pick as a controller. That's because she's a passive type. Her favorite ploy is to use personal praise to control people. She heaps such praise on people that they find it hard to disagree with her or to turn her down when she makes requests for their time and attention. In this way she takes advantage of others' goodwill. When she senses people pulling away, she pours it on even thicker.

Controllers usually have to be very forcefully challenged in order to change. Unless they come to grips with their lack of respect for other people and with the sources of their need for control, they will continue their controlling ways.

**Nonresponsives.**  Nonresponsives are leaders who have learned to deal with boundary issues by not responding to others' needs or problems. They have so walled themselves off that they are not drawn to alleviate others' suffering. Ministry roles don't usually attract nonresponsives, so the number of spiritual leaders with this true condition is fairly rare. If they do get into spiritual leadership, they usually don't last very long.

A clear exception is the case where nonresponsives are so insulated by an organization that the people they lead are basically unaware of their shortcoming (as, for example, when an unresponsive leader is surrounded by highly caring and responsive staff). People unmoved by others' needs typically require significant psychological coaching or therapy.

Clearly, boundary issues are serious matters for leaders. Self-aware leaders realize that these issues affect many different aspects of their leadership, such as time management, leadership focus, ministry intentionality, health of the church or organizational culture, appropriate responses to conflict, and genuine responsiveness to people's needs. Absent this awareness, the leader is left vulnerable to a variety of derailments, from being jerked around by others' expectations to being so highly controlling that they lose their own emotional presence to being uncaring about others. The price to pay for unexamined boundaries is too high.

## Personal Markers

Like markers in DNA that establish a person's key features, every leader has a set of personal markers (both positive and negative—even traumatic—experiences) that profoundly shape who the leader has become. Self-aware leaders learn to identify these markers and assess their impact on their life and leadership. Since the markers are as unique as the leader, it is impossible to note all of them. However, some fairly common markers inform the shaping dynamics of spiritual leaders.

### The Call

For spiritual leaders "the call" frames the central story line in their life dramas. Sometimes the call is dramatic, like Moses' burning bush experience or Paul's Damascus road encounter. For others the call is progressive, like David's long journey between the anointing at his father's house by Samuel and the anointing as king at Hebron by the elders. Either way, leaders center their lives, their vocation, and their location around the call. The call is not an added dimension to their journey; it gives meaning to the trip. It is personal. Spiritual leaders cannot be understood apart from their call because it tells them what game they are playing and keeps them in the game, even when they are discouraged.

Even more significantly, the leader's relationship with God is inextricably linked to the call. Moses knew Yahweh as the voice from the bush and the subsequent fire of Sinai. The Jesus that confronted Paul in the blinding light was the fulfillment of the Pharisee's messianic hopes—the Resurrected One, leading the apostle to frame his most personal desire this way: "That I may know him, and the power of his resurrection and the fellowship of sharing in his sufferings, becoming like him in his death" (Philippians 3:10, NIV).

Great leaders can detail their call. It is not guesswork for them, nor is it subject to revision, nor is it confined to a job description or the amount of salary it brings. Even though leaders sometimes wish they could escape the call (because of its demands), they center and order their lives around it. At the end of the day, they want to have been found faithful to fulfilling the call of God on their lives.

Jordan told her story to a group of seminarians. "Don't even think about a life in ministry unless you have a call." She went on, "But if you have a call, you'll be miserable doing anything else." Jordan recounted her journey into desperation as she slowly but surely grew disenchanted with the work she was doing on church staff. Even though she served a successful church, she felt they were largely keeping people busy in church activity but not actively transforming lives.

Eventually, she couldn't do it any longer. She called up an old friend she had been to school with and asked him for a job in the hospitality industry (after all, she understood catering to people's needs!). Her friend told Jordan she was making a mistake but wanted to help, so he signed her up for a position. However, Jordan told the class, her friend was right. Jordan was miserable— all because of "the call thing," as she put it. She returned to spiritual leadership but this time to a ministry position that more closely matched her personal values.

## God-Given Talent

Great spiritual leaders believe that they have been called, not *in spite* of who they are but *because of* who they are. This understanding is not a boast; rather, it is based on an honest assessment of their ability. Unlike many people and leaders who are naïve about their talent, self-aware leaders know what they are good at. They know what they bring to the table (and what they don't). This gives them permission to be intentional with their energies and time, always playing toward their talent. They do not practice wishful thinking when it comes to their abilities. They know their depth and take assignments that they can genuinely address with their skills and gifts.

> Walt should never have taken the offer. He simply didn't have the talent for it. Yet it was a move up in his denomination, so he felt he couldn't pass up the chance to take on a larger leadership role. Since his talent had matched his previous job requirements so well, Walt had shined! He had attracted the attention of the folks at headquarters, so they recruited him to a new position they were creating. Unfortunately, Walt's star fell when he could not measure up to the assignment. After a miserable two years, he finally moved into another role, much like the one he had excelled in previously. Unfortunately, the wrong move cost Walt dearly—financially, as well as in reputation. Had Walt been more aware of the limits of his capability and what he is really good at doing, he never would have fallen victim to the siren song of taking the "better" position.

Being self-aware about talent does not mean leaders do not have to be humble, which is also a central component of greatness. In fact, leaders in true possession of their strengths understand the source of their strengths. They attribute their accomplishments to the Giver of their abilities. Without this clear grasp, leaders dishonor their design and can end up working outside their strengths, whether out of ignorance or from an inflated ego that craves talent that didn't come from God. These leaders even become a liability by underperforming and by keeping other people from operating from their God-given strengths.

## Personal Traits

In addition to innate talents, leaders have other traits that are important parts of their personal markers. These include family relationships, temperament, personality, passions, and values, as well as a host of preferences in lifestyle and ministry. One key personal trait that should be explored is leaders' cognitive style. *Cognitive style* refers to how a leader processes information. Some leaders work better from rules and principles, whereas others prefer to connect their own dots from conceptual components. Some leaders think more in case-by-case situations, whereas others gravitate to the 40,000-foot view—thinking in terms of systems and movements. While some cognitive styles begin with the here and now, others start in the future. Many leaders withdraw into themselves when making decisions, whereas others need to talk things through with others in order to arrive at a decision.

The point of leaders' understanding their own cognitive styles is not just for self-knowledge but also to help leaders appreciate the preferences of others. Otherwise, they may tend to impose their own style of thinking on others, believing that others begin their thinking at the same point they do and process information the way they do. One leader who completed an assessment of his cognitive style chuckled as he observed, "Until I knew how my mind functioned and that other people's brains actually process things differently, I just thought those who disagreed with me were either obstinate or ignorant!" This proves the paradox again: the more self-aware leaders become, the greater their capacity to respect other people for who they are.

## Key Events in Life

This category of personal markers includes formative major events, successes and failures, and turning points in the leader's life. Key events may be positive or negative: significant encounters with God, separation or divorce of parents, death of a loved one, a great achievement, an educational milestone, a move to another part of the country or world, a failed marriage, being fired, or enduring a major conflict in ministry are just a few examples.

Reviewing and reflecting on these key events can help leaders connect the dots, recognizing God's providence across the years. Leaders can also realize how they have been shaped both by crises and by routine rhythms of life. This awareness can inspire confidence and provide comfort, especially to embattled leaders who need reminding that God has not abandoned them. Such an analysis can be conducted on one's own or in a group, which can help leaders see blind spots they might not have found on their own.

> At one retreat with a small group of ministry peers, Ruth, a young leader, shared stories of broken relationships and inter-personal conflicts. Ruth could explain each instance in terms of how others had disappointed and mistreated her. After hearing her story of a third failed staff experience, a concerned member of the group perceptively and gently asked, "Ruth, what have you figured out to be your contribution to each failure?" This question served to open Ruth's eyes and set her on a journey of self-discovery. She no longer views herself as a victim. Instead, seeing her own self-sabotaging behavior has enabled her to take charge of her next ministry chapter as a more whole person.

Great spiritual leaders have catalogued their positive and neg-ative personal markers and gleaned the heart-shaping work of God in them. This understanding inspires both humility and confidence.

## The Dark Side of Being a Leader

All leaders have a dark side, because every human being struggles with dysfunction to some degree. The dark sides of leaders are just more noticeable (to others more often than to themselves, unfor-tunately) because of the public scrutiny they receive and because of how their implications are amplified through their followers. Self-aware leaders come to grips with this dark part of themselves so they can take responsibility for it and learn to manage it. If they don't, they run the risk of becoming leaders whose leadership is charac-terized and shaped primarily by their dark side.

Gary McIntosh and Samuel Rima[2] identify five types of dark-side leaders: compulsive, narcissistic, paranoid, codependent, and passive-aggressive.

*Compulsive Leaders.*   Compulsive leaders need to maintain absolute order. They feel that the organization's performance directly reflects on them personally, so they implicate themselves into every possible part of the organization. They are typically very status conscious and are eager to please authority figures, from whom they need constant reassurance. Their outward order (grooming, clothing, speech, family, work environment) betrays an inner emotional turbulence. They are often angry, rebellious leaders who tend to be excessively critical of themselves and others.

*Narcissistic Leaders.*   Narcissistic leaders combine intense ambitiousness, overwhelming feelings of inferiority, and excessive needs for affirmation. Unsure of themselves, these leaders view anyone else's achievements as threats because they take the spotlight off the leaders' achievements. Narcissistic leaders use other people and ministry venues as ways to feel better about themselves. Their grandiose plans often are camouflaged with statements about faith and the greatness of God (especially if raising money is involved). No amount of accomplishment will fill these leaders' need for affirmation, nor can these leaders fill their own emotional deficit through relationships, because they use other people to further their own ambitions.

*Paranoid Leaders.*   Paranoid leaders are suspicious of others and therefore extremely guarded in their relationships. Because they are insecure, they are jealous of other gifted people. They tend to over-react to criticism and assume that any problems in the ministry organization pose a threat to them personally. These leaders sometimes conduct clandestine surveillance on other members of the team, even developing an extensive spy network in order to gather information that helps them stay in power. They may develop elaborate reporting mechanisms to keep themselves informed.

*Codependent Leaders.* Codependent people are often drawn to the ministry and to other helping professions out of a seemingly hard-wired tendency to be focused on others' actions and emotions at the expense of their own boundaries and emotional states. Consequently, they usually have a schedule that is out of control, overloaded with the cares of people in their ministry constituency. They often minister to others in order to feed their own need to be needed. Unchecked, this can lead to burnout.

*Passive-Aggressive Leaders.* Passive-aggressive leaders resist others' demands by procrastinating and by being stubborn and forgetful. If they choose to perform tasks that are expected of them, they do so with little enthusiasm, often feeling angry with those whom they perceive have forced them to work. Passive-aggressives on the one hand blame their failures on others' lack of support. Then if other people rally to them in supportive ways, these leaders claim that these same people are interfering with their leadership. Since passive-aggressive leaders can be irritable and impatient, they create an unstable environment in which people are on edge, waiting for the other shoe to drop.

If you recognize yourself in any of these patterns, be assured that others have noticed, too! Please get help. Your leadership is toxic to the people around you and to your organization. An able coach can clarify new behaviors to replace the current harmful ones. You may also want to choose a therapy route to deal with some psychological and emotional issues.

## Destructive Patterns of Leadership

The dark side of leaders may take more forms than just the ones that McIntosh and Rima describe. David Dotlich and Peter Cairo[3] also detail specific derailing behavior of leaders that draw on the dark side. They observe that leaders act, speak, and think in ways that often cause them to fail, often without even realizing they are doing this to themselves. These consultants identify eleven derailing patterns:

arrogance, melodramatic behavior, volatility, excessive caution, habitual mistrust, aloofness, mischievousness, eccentricity, passive resistance, perfectionism, and excessive eagerness to please.

After his third melt-down in as many months, Hal finally confronted his dark side, with the help of a ministry supervisor who insisted on it and a colleague who agreed to serve as a coach and accountability partner. Hal's pattern involved outbursts with coworkers, followed by tearful apologies in which he blamed family stresses and work pressures for his misbehavior. In his journey toward understanding his dark side, Hal came to realize he had a combination of melodramatic behavior, coupled with perfectionism. To subordinates he came across as arrogant, even abusive. This was hidden to superiors, because with them Hal was always eager to please.

To his credit Hal threw himself into himself as a priority project. He identified situations and circumstances that made him more susceptible to acting out. He made a list of behaviors that needed changing. He agreed to a weekly accountability session where his week would be reviewed. Even more significantly, he agreed to receive regular feedback from his entire leadership constellation, those above him as well as those below him in the organizational food chain. These quarterly feedbacks would form the basis of his performance review. Behavioral patterns like Hal's do not go away immediately. He had relapses. But his commitment to improvement earned Hal the grace from others to allow him time and room to grow.

Dark-side leadership is harder to challenge if it has been coddled or nurtured by a dysfunctional organization. "I have a problem," the new pastor confided during a seminar. "The worship leader in our congregation routinely launches into tirades with people. Just this week he lit into me." The startled pastor found out that this behavior had been going on for twenty years. "That's just Noah," people told him. When asked why the congregation put up with this outrageous behavior, the pastor replied that Noah was an excellent worship leader. In essence, the congregation had enabled Noah's dark side because in the end he gave them what they wanted. This pastor's chance of successfully confronting this well-entrenched leader was slim.

The dark sides of leaders inevitably are exposed to those they lead; they are hard to miss. And the leaders are difficult and dysfunctional to be around. But leaders who are captive to such darkness may not become acquainted with it enough so they can manage it. And so the dark side manages them. Great spiritual leaders understand that becoming acquainted with the dark is the only path to the light.

## The Price of Lack of Self-Awareness

If the path to self-awareness sounds long and arduous, full of insights that you may be thinking you'd rather not have to face, it's worth keeping in mind that there is a price to be paid for the failure to gain significant self-awareness. Neither alternative is good—for leaders or for those who follow them. Both alternatives keep leaders from freely giving themselves in service to other people.

One option is the hollow leader—a person with no sense of self, a person who works only from the expectations of others. Since such leaders have no inner core, no authenticity, they merely play a role of being a leader. Hollow leaders hand over the verification of their lives and ministry to others because there is no one home. They are functionaries.

The other danger of a lack of self-awareness is leaders who are so self-absorbed that they are unaware of others' needs. For self-absorbed leaders, it's all about them. In every situation their primary concern is about how they are being treated, how they are affected, how they look, how they are responding. They minister to others to get their own needs met. They are still in search of self.

---

Self-awareness is not automatic in spiritual leaders. It can't be assumed. It only comes to those leaders who see themselves as appropriate and crucial fields of study. A spiritual leader does not arrive at self-awareness all at once. The learning about self may be jumpstarted or accelerated by precipitous events or challenges that thrust the leader into an inner journey. In a normal progression, the learning curve is typically steeper early on, as the leader grapples with early leadership assignments and life passages. However, not all leaders work on self-awareness in their early years. For some it is postponed until later life. "I didn't come alive until I was sixty," one leader recently confided in me. Up until that time he was working off of a borrowed leadership template, trying to be someone he was not. He is now free indeed and having the time of his life. He proves that it is never too late to learn more about oneself. But it is also never too early to start!

What are you waiting for? Greatness is waiting for you!

# 2

# THE DISCIPLINE OF
# SELF-MANAGEMENT

Carl lost it. The lava flow that had been building up inside him for months suddenly erupted. He told the group of assembled elders exactly what he thought of their criticisms of how he had handled a staff exit. Following his tirade he stomped out of the meeting, leaving a lot of stunned people seated around the table. That's not all Carl left behind that night. His explosion knocked the luster off years of leadership.

Sarah was brilliant. Everyone knew it, including Sarah. As a result she routinely flashed her impatience with people who didn't "get it." Slow to listen and quick to speak, Sarah gained a reputation of being hard to get along with. She also gained a lot of employment history full of the same drama: fast start, toxic finish.

The first leader lost his emotional cool. The second failed to exhibit emotional intelligence. Unfortunately, these two examples do not begin to exhaust the ways that leaders can either reduce their effectiveness or lose it altogether. Some spiritual leaders are haunted by expectations; others are fearful that their poor money habits will be discovered. Still others struggle with success, while others wrestle with failure. All of these situations have a common denominator: mismanagement by the leader.

Great leaders are great managers—not just managers of projects or other people but mostly of themselves. They understand that the pressures of external circumstances are not the likely potholes that will cause the wheels to come off their leadership vehicle or even sideline them with a blowout. They know that internal self-management of their own mental, emotional, and spiritual health is the key.

Some essential things that spiritual leaders must manage are common to leaders of all enterprises; others are special challenges for those who lead in the spiritual arena. The discussion that follows highlights areas that prove most critical for spiritual leaders to manage and offers some strategies for doing so.

## Managing Feelings

Emotions just happen. They are neither good nor bad in themselves. It's what we do with emotions that counts in terms of self-management. The key to emotional health is not to deny emotions. Just the opposite is true. Leaders must learn to own their emotions so they can manage them rather than let emotions be in charge.

A few emotions prove problematic enough to merit special attention. Volumes have been written on each of the ones discussed here, but my intention is to raise awareness for further investigation if you see yourself particularly vulnerable to any of the following emotions that frequently challenge leaders' self-management.

### Depression

Technically speaking, depression is not an emotion. Yet this condition influences so many emotions that it makes sense to deal with it here, especially because this dragon that terrorizes so many people in our culture seems especially fond of preying on spiritual leaders. The kinds of issues and situations that ministers deal with, combined with the overwhelming desire to help people (a psychological component of many people drawn into the helping professions, including the ministry), brew the conditions conducive to depression. This is why Archibald Hart, former dean of the School of Psychology at Fuller Seminary, often says that surviving the ministry is a matter of surviving depression.

People suffer from two types of depression. The first is *endogenous depression*, which is biological in nature and requires medication (usually antidepressants) for treatment. People suffering with this depression typically feel worse in the morning. Usually, this means that endogenously depressed persons feel better at night and want to stay up because they dread the morning. Therapy is not a cure for endogenous depression but can help the afflicted person cope with troubled emotions. Breakthroughs in medicine have helped many people address this type of depression, which affects and alters the behavior of people who suffer with it.

A second type of depression—*exogenous depression*—is a psychological and emotional condition that is usually a response to some loss. The loss can be anything, from the death of a loved one to a crushed expectation. The response may involve only relatively minor mood swings to more significant emotions. Medication is only a partial answer for exogenous depression. It can provide for symptomatic relief; however, over time, no medication will help exogenous depression. The best treatment is at the emotional and psychological level. Often a skilled therapist can help exogenously depressed people identify their problems and can coach them to emotional health. Distractions (like vacations or entertainment), physical rest, and exercise help. Exogenous depression will pass if active steps are taken to allow for appropriate grieving and restorative practices. This is a normal emotional reaction to life's downers.

Both types of depression evidence some classic symptoms, including confused thinking, a loss of interest in work or hobbies, inertia, fear of losing one's mind, feelings of impotence, appetite shifts in either direction, sleep-pattern shifts, guilt, and stomach discomfort. The presence of one or two of these symptoms does not, in itself, signal depression; we all have an occasional sleepless night or have indigestion after eating too much pizza. However, if you are experiencing a number of these symptoms, particularly several of the first items in the list, you should talk to your doctor or go see a trusted counselor for a medical and psychological checkup. Don't play doctor and self-diagnose!

Many more spiritual leaders battle depression than realize it. The longer pastor Barry talked to me, the more it was obvious he was battling depression. The trouble was, he thought he was just tired and failing in his spiritual life because he was feeling "defeated" (a misdiagnosis that ministers often make). When I went down the list of symptoms with him, we discovered he was experiencing almost every one. Once he realized what he was really up against, Barry wisely sought medical and psychological help.

## Anger

The common emotion of anger plagues many spiritual leaders, just as it does everyone else. All humans experience anger. Even Jesus got angry—at the Pharisees, at the money changers in the temple, even at his own disciples. Anger is a psychological response of readiness, usually caused by hurt, fear, or frustration. The hurt that elicits an angry response can be physical or emotional. Feeling irritated, misunderstood, violated, maligned—all these emotions can produce anger for spiritual leaders.

Fear also threatens spiritual leaders: fear of alienation or the loss of income or esteem or position. These concerns can cause a flood of anger in leaders. Disappointment with life station, blocked goals, or unrealistic expectations that cannot possibly be met often contribute to high frustration levels that lead to anger among spiritual leaders. It is not a sin to respond with anger. The key is to be angry but not sin (Ephesians 4:26).

Great leaders learn to manage their anger. They adopt several key strategies to help them with this. They identify what pushes their hot buttons and why (fears, disappointments, threats, and so on). They don't allow themselves to indulge in poor learned responses (like tantrums). These leaders choose not to let anger fester, knowing this sets them up for failure. If they have problems with angry behavior, they have made themselves accountable by giving those around them permission to "check" them when their anger begins to manifest itself.

Unfortunately, anger is often mismanaged. Some leaders explode emotionally. Others act in a punitive or retaliatory way. Still others somatize their anger, actually visiting it on themselves in elevated blood pressure, headaches, body aches, and stomach problems. Mismanaged anger always exacts a price, either in the leader's relationships, health, or capacity to lead.

The two leaders in the opening of this chapter chose different responses to address their anger. Carl sought spiritual direction and counsel. Over time he repaired his leadership. Sarah has ignored her responsibility, still blaming others. She is bewildered as to why she never advances in her leadership potential.

## Hostility

Psychologists have long recognized that individuals vary in the degree to which they harbor and express hostile and antagonistic attitudes and behavior. Many leaders who are filled with hostility seem unaware of the way they come across: finding fault and being hard-to-please, critical, judgmental, insensitive, and caustic. They seldom stop to ask the kinds of questions that would reveal their hostility for what it is.

Do others frequently annoy you? Do you often speak of changes others need to make? Do you frequently make disparaging remarks about others' behavior and appearance? For leaders who answer these questions with a yes, this could mark the beginning of self-awareness of hostile attitudes and tendencies.

Several factors are known to feed hostility: unresolved anger and personal self-esteem issues (that is, the hostile person is not happy with himself or herself) and unrealistic expectations (both for the leader and for others). Hostile leaders often reflect an internal performance standard that torments them. Subconsciously, they often tear other people down in an attempt to make themselves feel better by comparison. Of course, this activity never produces the hoped-for elevation of self-esteem.

If you suspect that you may have a problem with hostility, it's not hard to find out for sure. Just ask those around you if you are a hostile person. Though they'll have no doubt if you are, they may be reluctant to tell you the truth, for fear of facing more of your hostility. This is why dealing with hostility requires self-awareness. The leader has to come out of denial and start trying to figure out what he or she was trying to achieve by being so hostile and critical.

The process of introspection will also need to probe what influences from the past may be contributing to this hostility. Leaders may need to forgive some perceived or real hurt. The process of self-examination will then have to be followed by an intentional effort to replace poor behaviors associated with hostility with conscious efforts to praise more, criticize less, and practice patience. Leaders who recognize their hostile ways may need to seek new companions. Because hostile people sometimes hang together, choosing grace-filled people as companions may soften the leader's hostility and provide new models of how to lead without criticism and antagonism.

Makeisha finally figured out that her own hostility was to blame for broken relationships in her life, including the people who had once been in her leadership circle. After making the painful admission to herself that she was toxic in organizations, she sought out a skilled therapist who helped her uncover the underlying causes for her hostility. Makeisha's determination to bless others rather than to curse them (through her hostility) sustained a courageous journey to confront the internal dragons that were terrorizing her. She discovered that her outward hostility belied a very fearful, insecure person.

## Grief and Loss

Grief is a healthy emotion, designed to help us deal with loss. One's level of faith affects the outcome of the grief process but neither the need to grieve nor the time required to do it. Spiritual leaders, like everyone else—and sometimes even more than others—encounter their share of grief and loss. Friends are sometimes lost as a result of leadership decisions. Leaders and their families may also lose money as a result of taking a leadership assignment (discretionary losses are still losses). Separation from family and friends can also occur, especially if moving around is part of the leader's journey. Yet many spiritual leaders do not claim their own need to grieve. They are so often on the front line of helping others deal with their losses that they sometimes neglect their own.

Leaders need to express their pain of grief and loss. Suffering in silence is a Stoic, not Christian, notion. "Stuffing" pain is not a sign of emotional maturity; in fact, just the opposite is true. Jesus wept at Lazarus's tomb. The Son of God knew that sorrow is passing and that joy is forever, yet it did not prevent him from standing in his grief when that was the emotion that arose.

> The executive leadership team and governing board met for the first time since the founding pastor had abruptly retired after a run-in with several board members. Ostensibly, the meeting was called to begin forging a new alliance between staff and board. New structures and pathways were needed because the founding pastor's model had been to isolate the two groups. Palpable suspicion and pain hung like heavy curtains over the group as they convened. The retreat leader began by asking everyone to identify their grief. Shocked at first, several members finally understood that the anger they felt toward the departed pastor was part of the grief process, as was the despondency of others. These high-octane leaders were unaware of their own grief, much less that of others.

Appropriate grieving involves expressing the pain of loss, not burying it. It reviews and rehearses the loss; it doesn't just move to replace the loss with something new. Good grief takes place in community, not just in solitude. Unshared grief arrests the healing. Of course, time alone does not heal. God heals.

## Fear

The e-mail came to me just minutes before I was leaving to go out of the country. Its contents called into question some leadership direction I was giving to a futuring group that was working to determine our denomination's future. The writer included veiled threats about what would happen if I continued with the plans we were making. Three days later, even on another continent, I found myself still stewing about the e-mail. I had composed dozens of responses in my mind for when I returned. I was building up quite a head of steam until I realized the role that fear was playing in my reaction. My wife was the source of discovery when she asked, "What if the e-mail is right? Is losing your job the worst thing that can happen to us?" Suddenly, I realized that fear was the primal emotion that triggered my anger. Once the dragon was called out, it lost its power to intimidate. Upon returning home I had a very unanxious discussion with the e-mail author (we still didn't agree, but I did not respond to him out of anger).

Many spiritual leaders are racked by fear—fear of losing leadership, fear of losing income, fear of losing favor, fear of not being obedient to God, fear of not realizing dreams. The enemy of our souls loves to whisper fear in our ears. Whenever a spiritual leader deals with fear, the source is sure. Fear keeps many spiritual leaders from proclaiming truth and leading with courage. God understands our fear. "Don't be afraid" is an oft-repeated statement in the scriptures. Frequently, it is joined by the promise of God's presence (which, since it is perfect love, casts out fear).

Yet, like all the other emotions we are discussing here, fear can be managed. Leaders can take actions to combat or to release their fears. The beginning is identifying the source of the fear so that, once named, it can more easily be faced. Leaders can also gain strength by sharing their fears with others. We gain power and courage when we know we are not alone. Sometimes leaders must face the fear squarely in order to break its hold. Imagine the worst that can happen. Run out the scenarios. Then remember that God will still be present and working, no matter what.

## Bitterness

Bitterness that takes the form of disappointment, resentment, or cynicism is one of the most pernicious negative emotions that spiritual leaders have to confront. It is also one that can keep us far from achieving greatness, as well as joy, in our lives. Bitterness is a cancer of the spirit. Though its roots and expression may differ from individual to individual, it unfailingly eats away at emotional, spiritual, even physical health. The people of God are not aided in their journey by the spirit of bitterness, nor can the hand of God stay with a leader full of bitterness.

Bitterness, like hostility, is fed by others' emotions. It is as if a consortium of beasts conspires to implant bitterness in spiritual leaders. Depression may lay the foundation. Mismanaged anger can open a doorway to its entrance, while hostility can lead to increased bitterness. Some great loss that is not properly grieved can anesthetize leaders to the sting of bitterness. Fear can trap a leader into not doing (or doing) certain things, which then begins a cycle of self-doubt that can lead to self-incrimination or even self-loathing, as the leader despises his own perceived lack of courage. Such emotions often lead to bitterness in the leader.

> Alex never recovered from being passed over for the promotion in his ministry organization. Over time his anger turned to hostility toward his superiors. He wasted no opportunity to criticize the organization and its leaders. When he realized that others did not share his views or take up his call, his frustration level increased and his spirit became even darker. After several confrontations and warnings about his attitude, Alex was fired.

Leaders who fight the dragon of bitterness successfully wage an all-out investigation into its source, including not just events and people but the emotional run-off we have already mentioned. Then they rigorously practice forgiveness, which applies antiseptic treatment to the infection of their soul. Unconquered, bitterness will disqualify leaders and rob them of the requisite spiritual power they must have to conduct ministry.

## Managing Expectations

Along with managing emotions, leaders have to learn to manage their expectations of themselves and of others. Expectations, like emotions, are normal and natural; the trick is to set them at the appropriate level. Three sets of expectations demand attention: (1) your expectations of yourself, (2) others' expectations of you, and (3) expectations that you, as a leader, have concerning your followers.

### Expectations of Yourself

Great leaders expect a lot of themselves, but they refuse to let their shortcomings hold them back. They know that personal expectations must be sufficiently nurtured to motivate but not allowed to become crushing when they go unmet. Self-awareness helps leaders learn to calibrate their self-expectations. Self-understanding informs leaders of their talent potential, their personality strengths, their physical abilities—all important when establishing what situations they are suited for and ill-suited for.

Great leaders do not engage in self-flagellation when they disappoint themselves. They are not afflicted with an inflated view of themselves, believing they would never fail. "I know there are things I could have done differently," Ron said, when we met after his termination. "The important thing is to learn from this experience and to move on." This healthy perspective keeps Ron from putting himself on the rack, furthering weakening his leadership confidence.

### Others' Expectations of You

Too many spiritual leaders do not understand the critical importance of being in touch with followers' expectations of them. The twin risks here are for the leader to disregard these expectations, on the one hand, or to be captured or determined by them on the other. Both ends of the spectrum can be deadly. Ignoring expectations will convince followers that the leader is uninterested in them. People who feel uncared for become disaffected pretty quickly. As I am writing these lines, the victims of hurricane Katrina are not too happy with the federal government—FEMA (Federal Emergency Management Agency) in particular—for the response to their plight.

Yet leaders cannot hand control over their expectations to followers. This leads to a form of enmeshment that ultimately sets the leader up for failure. Leaders who are psychologically dependent on their followers for their own sense of self-esteem and self-worth create an unhealthy dynamic. These leaders actually cannot separate themselves from their followers enough to give leadership.

Truthfully, managing expectations is an art form, with no set formulas. Every leader knows there are times to yield to expectations of followers in order to achieve the leadership capital they need to achieve some goal or to accomplish some project. However, over the long haul a leader must do more to shape followers' expectations than merely to meet them. Expectations should be in line with the organization's mission and the leader's personal makeup, including his or her own individual mission, talent, passion, and personality. A leader who shapes expectations remains healthier than one who is primarily shaped by them. Those who feel driven by others' expectations may feel trapped or feel they have lost control. Either way, the result makes them susceptible to emotional burnout.

Jayne never felt that she performed up to her leadership potential in her congregational role. Her denomination largely restricted the expression of leadership in women to children's or women's ministries. Jayne felt that the static expectations of this culture prevented her from exploring her leadership potential. She joined a parachurch ministry that gave her greater freedom in crafting her leadership role—a place of service where she could shape the expectations of others, based on the full range of her talent. She is a much happier camper.

Andy decided he'd shape the congregation's expectations of him, beginning in the prospective visits by the pastor search team. He informed them of his gifts and passions, as well as those things he felt he was not well equipped to do. He took a further step when meeting with the entire prospective congregation.

Too many spiritual leaders, either due to a lack of personal confidence or because of misguided perfectionism, are too eager to please. Consequently, they fail to shape their followers' expectations about their performance and leadership.

## The Leader's Expectations of Followers

Setting and communicating expectations for followers is just as demanding and important as the other kinds of expectations we have discussed. Great leaders inspire people by calling them to do more than they think they are capable of. Less-than-great leaders create environments in which followers fail to measure up—and know it.

Very few staff leaders left serving with Wesley unscathed by the experience. His demands were unreasonable. He was never fully satisfied with results, always pushing for more. He would often obsess over details that made little difference in outcomes. What Wesley called "excellence" was in reality a pathology-based leadership that made his coworkers sick.

Others coerce and intimidate their followers into meeting their expectations.

When Roger couldn't get what he wanted through manipulation or sweet talk, he resorted to yelling and threats. He could appear lighthearted and even solicitous until someone disagreed with him; then he quickly became menacing and verbally abusive. Followers were often taken off guard (and some badly shaken) by his sudden change in demeanor.

Still other leaders who want to be liked or who are unwilling to risk any disharmony or tension go too far to another extreme, thus lowering the bar on expectations to the point where they fail to create a culture of achievement or excellence.

Harry's dark side of leadership was his need for approval. Consequently, he tolerated all manner of incompetence for fear of confronting someone. The congregation he led suffered for it. People were recruited to leadership positions but never coached for effectiveness. The only ministries that performed well were those lucky enough to be headed by high-octane leaders who needed little instruction or management. Yet these leaders were often hindered by the poor work of others—a key source of the discontent and low morale resulting in constant leadership turnover on Harry's team.

## Staying Healthy

Spiritual leaders deal with matters of the heart and soul, but sometimes they forget that their physical hearts need tending and protecting, as do other body organs and systems that are a part of the temple of the Spirit. Great leaders take as much care of themselves physically as they do other emotional and spiritual aspects. It makes sense to do so from a practical standpoint, since practicing good health habits reduces the hassles and hindrances inherent in physical limitations, as well as prevents premature incapacitation or even death. Each of us operates with certain physical givens: body shapes, metabolic rates, congenital factors, genetic predispositions toward certain diseases, and health problems that pose unique challenges to physical health management. Other health challenges, of course, result from the leader's lifestyle choices.

I do not mean to suggest here that exceptional leaders must always enjoy exceptional health. Many great leaders have suffered from significant health problems. Franklin Delano Roosevelt's polio did not disqualify him from being a great president. Neither did Paul's thorn in the flesh (many suspect it was a nagging medical condition) prevent him from achieving greatness in spiritual leadership. However, leaders must pay attention to the physical requirements of leadership by eating right, exercising, and getting adequate sleep (sleep deprivation has been linked to heart problems and even obesity, not to mention irritability, fuzzy thinking, and lack of judgment).

Fred consistently pushed the envelope where his body was concerned. His style was to practice unhealthy choices (overeat, undersleep, overexert) and go into hyper-drive until his body would demand its due. This reckoning usually took the form of some kind of physical crash about every month (illness, stomach problems, exhaustion) that took him out of commission a few days. This pattern eventually cost Fred his high-level position of leadership in his ministry organization. He essentially became too undependable and erratic in his work performance. Too many people were inconvenienced each time he drove himself over the edge.

Susan was diagnosed with adult-onset diabetes. A brilliant consultant and strategist and a tireless worker, she had created a substantial portfolio of clients. Unfortunately, Susan refused to accept the new diet and rest requirements of her medical condition. She denied them and even adopted destructive behaviors as if to challenge the disease. She planned more road trips, increased her work load, ate all the wrong foods, and refused to exercise (blaming her road schedule and work load). The result? She no longer has the client load. And she's off the road. The diabetes she denied is now running her life.

Leaders need to understand that followers are not drawn toward leaders who do not take care of themselves. In an age of increased awareness of health issues, followers do not respect leaders who fail to practice physical self-management.

## Staying Mentally Vibrant

Great leaders stay sharp mentally. They realize that to stay engaged and growing requires that they maintain their brains. Leaders can promote healthy brain chemistry by paying attention to some key concerns.

- *Adequate sleep.* Research is continuing to establish the correlation between adequate sleep and physiological health and resiliency. A sleep-hungry brain is subject to fuzzy thinking, poor judgment, and worry. One leader who came to see me was almost paralyzed with worry over his leadership situation. After listening to him detail his concerns, I simply asked him how much sleep he had been getting. He admitted that he had gone several weeks without a good night's sleep. What he had not realized was that his sleep deprivation was feeding this toxic worry.
- *Proper diet.* When it comes to feeding our brains, protein is important. Spiritual leaders who start their day with sugars and carbohydrates will not send much nourishment upstairs. For those who speak in front of crowds and wish to have something to say, I suggest some form of protein be chosen for breakfast rather than doughnut holes.
- *Moderate use of alcohol, caffeine, nicotine.* These are ways we typically "medicate" our anxieties.
- *Adequate exercise.* This is not only good for our own physical bodies; it is essential for brain maintenance. Not only do the brain hormones called endorphins released through exercise create a sense of well-being; they also create a frame of mind for the leader that promotes positive perspectives and good judgment.
- *Daily doses of positive human contact.* Well-known studies chronicle the severe impact of a loss of human contact on newborn babies, including all sorts of physical problems (even death), as well

as the emotional trauma of a failure to bond with other humans physically. Adults do not outgrow this need (witness the studies of senior adult populations in nursing homes that demonstrate the positive impact of physical contact and the withering effects of isolation). Leaders who are connected and enjoying positive human contact (physical and emotional) are keeping their brains wired for positive thoughts—a mind-set that is critical to greatness in spiritual leadership. There is no wonder that Jesus chose to spend his last weekend on earth before initiating his passion by hanging out at the home of Mary, Martha, and Lazarus, his three closest friends.

• *Mental recreation*. Brain fatigue is fairly common in a world where we are constantly in-touch, online, accessible, "out there." Leaders need time for their brains to rest between sets. Otherwise, their thinking becomes dull and tired. Different leaders enjoy different things for mental rest: hobbies, sports, movies, reading, travel. Leaders need to figure out what works for them. Then just do it.

• *Muse time*. Donald Clifton, the late CEO of The Gallup Organization, always challenged the participants in his Leadership Institute to build adequate "muse time" into their schedules. By that he meant time to ponder, to noodle, to reflect, to put our brains to work on items more critical than today's to-do list. The brain doesn't work on complex leadership issues in a linear, time-scripted manner. Insights often claw their way to the surface and pop out when unexpected. Great leaders tend to this incubation and birth process by setting aside time for it. No one hands leaders this time. They have to carve it out and protect it.

## Avoiding Brain Drains

In addition to cultivating the positive habits that promote excellent brain functioning, effective leaders know they have to avoid those people and situations that sap their mental health. Three "brain killers" deserve special attention: (1) negative people, (2) disorganization, and (3) second-guessing decisions.

• *Negative people*. Leaders need to be aware that when they allow themselves to be consumed by negative people (who seem so often inclined to seek them out), they allow precious mental, emotional, and spiritual energy to be drained off from other leadership pursuits. Obviously, leaders cannot totally avoid negative people, but they can deflect their negativity by creating a mental boundary. So acknowledge their destructive, energy-sapping perspective, and stay on your side of the wall. And adopt a strategy of surrounding yourself with positive people as a proactive strategy.

• *Disorganization*. Disorganization is a major brain drain. Not only does it consume time ("it's right here—somewhere") but it also raises anxiety ("what am I forgetting?"), which is another major cause of brain drain. Even leaders who do not count administration as a strength can be sure they don't sabotage their efforts through a lack of organization. They do this by recruiting someone to help them, by availing themselves of technology, and deciding to expend enough personal effort to get sufficiently organized.

This discussion is not intended to make you feel guilty for finding organization to be a challenge. The idea here is not that you get your desk completely clean or that you match the organizational skills of someone who has great propensity for this. You just want to defend against having a level of disorganization that creates a brain drain. Of course, some disorganized people don't even know this is a problem for them. Their way of life just feels normal to them. You can check this by asking your administrative assistant or a coworker who has exposure to your work habits to tell you if disorganization is something you should work on.

• *Tendency to second-guess decisions*. Some spiritual leaders waste energy when they allow nagging doubts, compounded by self-blame, to dog them if things don't go the way they anticipated when they made a decision. Depending on personality and cognitive style, leaders need differing amounts of information and lead times in order to make decisions. But once decisions are made, the best leaders practice little second-guessing. "Would I have made the same decision with the same information I had at the time?" is a good question for leaders to ask themselves when tempted to second-guess. If the answer is yes, then the leader can move on. If the answer is no, then the issue is to find a better way to make decisions (a topic for discussion in Chapter Five).

## Responding to Temptations

A new follower of Jesus once exclaimed to me, "It must be great for you not to be tempted as much as I am." He assumed that my maturity as a Jesus-follower and my role as a spiritual leader inoculated me against serious temptation. But nothing could be farther from reality. Every spiritual leader knows that the temptations get more insidious, perhaps more subtle, even more deadly as time goes on. In fact, exercising spiritual leadership sets a person up for greater temptations than the average bear! The reason for this phenomenon certainly lies in the potential downside of leaders when they fall, not that spiritual leaders are by nature somehow more susceptible to temptation. It has less to do with the leader than with the impact on his or her followers. The forces of evil get better return on investment when a leader falls.

We all know too many leaders who have cheated themselves out of potential greatness because of poor moral choices or addictive behaviors that eventually limited their influence or disqualified them to lead altogether. The list of temptations is fairly common: lust, power, pride, illicit sex, money, pornography, drug addiction, approval addiction. All sing their siren songs in every generation, calibrated to the leader's propensities and vulnerabilities.

Yet temptations come in other categories than just moral choices or character challenges. Many leaders, for instance, may not consider discouragement a temptation. But it is. Many leaders welcome discouragement too readily and play with it too long, feeling that they can afford it. Every leader faces discouragement; even great leaders do. But great leaders move past it, while other, lesser leaders turn discouragement into a pet or lifelong companion. They nurture it, all the while failing to see that they are aiding and abetting the enemy when they choose discouragement as company for extended stays. Feeling discouraged is perfectly normal—a part of grief in any healthy person. However, the "right" to be discouraged is a seductive force designed to take the leader out of play.

Another frequent temptation that leaders rarely recognize as such is distraction. This is a favorite ploy of the enemy of the leader's soul. The distraction doesn't usually come on as something evil or bad. The leader is just tempted to do more, or to waste time, or to squander his talent by failing to develop it, or to go stale by ignoring what it takes to care for himself mentally or emotionally. In fact, distractions can be composed of things that are good in themselves, yet the impact on the leader who is distracted is diminished effectiveness. Yielding to distraction prohibits many leaders from moving toward their greatness as leaders.

One leader failed to realize that his "missions heart" proved to be a distraction, when his globe trotting repeatedly took him out of the country at critical periods during his attempt to lead his congregation in an expansion phase. His absence (attending to a good thing overseas) cost him the ability to realize his dream for the congregation stateside. The window of opportunity passed, and the church entered a gradual slide that eventually bankrupted the leader's line of credit with many church members.

## Combating Temptation

Spiritual leaders need to adopt several strategies in combating temptations. None of this is rocket science, nor is there some magic pill to immunize leaders against temptations. Unfortunately, temptations, like viruses, constantly mutate their appeal in their quest to maximize their virulent potency. Just when a leader thinks a temptation has been conquered, it finds a new way to attack the leader's mind and spirit. This is why the following strategies to battle temptations should never be set aside or ignored. A leader needs them all.

• *Flee temptation.* Dieters know to stay out of the candy store. It's just that simple. Smart leaders know they are being chased, so they keep their running shoes on. They avoid places and situations that set them up to be tempted. They don't turn on the movie channel in the hotel room if they find they want to watch the wrong stuff; they don't go to the bar if that's a problem for them; they don't hang out with people who encourage negative emotions. Leaders can reduce their number of temptations by outrunning a bunch of them.

• *Dialogue with God about temptation.* The scriptures are pretty plain about this. We ask God to give us the power to withstand temptation. Unfortunately, we often fail to cash in on this promise because we don't talk to God about this part of our lives. Jesus even included this area of discussion in his Model Prayer. Intriguingly, we will often discuss our sins with God, but not our temptations. If we spoke more with him about the latter, we could reduce our need for conversation about the former. Why not go ahead and admit your temptation to God? Don't you think he knows about it already? It's amazing what insights might be available to us, as well as resources that give us the strength to endure.

• *Be accountable.* Who can the leader be open with about temptations? Apparently, Jesus was open about his, or we'd never have known about his experiences in the wilderness. The leader should ask himself who has the permission to give him a checkup or coach him in this area. Does the leader have a safe place and an appropriate venue for dealing with his temptations? Not everyone in a leader's constellation can qualify for this assignment, but someone should.

• *Gather good intelligence.* Know your nemesis and know where and when you are most vulnerable. One leader apologized for losing his temper with me, citing his physical tiredness. "I am learning," he said, "to simply shut up when I am tired. It would keep me from having to make phone calls like this." Some leaders notice they are more susceptible to temptation following great spiritual victories.

The Bible is full of those stories: Elijah after Carmel melts under the threat from Jezebel; Jesus faces Satan right after his public baptism and vocal blessing from his Father. Whose company opens you up to greater temptation? When should you not be alone? The point is to learn as much as possible about the rhythms and the character of the temptations you face.

I do not mean for any of this discussion to imply that the presence of temptations in the life of the spiritual leader signals failure. In fact, just the opposite may be true, particularly on the occasion of significant spiritual engagement. Great leaders do not expect to expunge temptation from their lives. They do not fall victim to an insidious perfectionism that robs them of authenticity. Instead, they acknowledge their temptations and proactively manage this aspect of their lives.

## Developing Emotional Intelligence

Bill possessed great gifts. He was entrepreneurial, highly intuitive in his ability to know things before others did, a compelling communicator, and tireless worker. But he was also distrustful, highly competitive, and given to a high need for control. He created a leadership culture that reflected his worst qualities. The board didn't trust the staff; the staff didn't trust the board. All lines of communication ran straight to Bill, who played people off, one against the other. Teamwork suffered because people basically needed only to please Bill, who was capricious in his praise and reward. Bill has low emotional intelligence (among other challenges).

Everyone wanted to be on Sally's team. She had fun with herself, her coworkers, and her constituents. She trusted people, was available to them when they needed her help, and was generous in her affirmation of good work. People flourished under her leadership.

Sally had high emotional intelligence that, combined with her high competency, made her a very effective leader.

Behavioral scientist and journalist Daniel Goleman[4] contends that only one-third of a leader's effectiveness lies in the areas of raw intelligence and technical expertise. The other two-thirds comprise the dimensions of what Goleman calls emotional intelligence, which include qualities such as self-awareness, impulse control, persistence, zeal, self-motivation, and empathy. The leader and his followers both benefit from this particular set of leadership competencies. The emotionally intelligent leader displays courage, self-control, and confidence, which establishes the basis for integrity, conscientiousness, and trustworthiness—all critical elements that followers look for. The leader's emotional intelligence is reflected in the leader's mood (optimistic or pessimistic), the leader's capacity for empathy (the ability to read emotions in others), and the leader's degree of connectedness with his followers.

Leaders' emotional intelligence carries huge implications for the organizations they lead because it mirrors the leaders' moods. Just as people have emotional connections between each other (this is why moods are contagious, especially laughter), organizations "catch" the emotional outlook of the leader. Leaders' enthusiasm, optimism, and energy ripple throughout their leadership constellation. Conversely, their discouragement, pessimism, and negativity also affect their followers. The leader sets the tone: upbeat, anxious, relaxed, stressed—whatever. That is why leaders must closely monitor the emotional signals they send out. Interestingly, "positive emotional IQ" has been linked to greater productivity in customer service organizations. People who serve others simply do a better job when they are satisfied emotionally with their work. Customers report better service. The implications for organizations targeting spiritual pursuits become obvious. If the mission is to engage people in ways that attract them to spiritual growth, a higher sense of emotional well-being among the ministry "workers" is required. This raises the bar for the leader who needs to develop and manage a high degree of emotional intelligence, both personally and in key leadership positions. The mission, in part, depends on it.

## Managing Money

Steve told me a painful story when we met:

> Steve was in serious financial trouble. All his credit cards were maxed out. He had borrowed two months of salary from the church, and the money had run out again with two weeks still left to go before the next check. He was embarrassed and demoralized— not the ingredients requisite for robust leadership. To make matters worse, his wife's overspending was the real culprit, so dealing with his financial woes was going to require his facing some stiff marital headwinds.

The issue of money management for leaders goes well beyond the realm of poor choices and undisciplined spending habits that contribute to financial woes. The issue here is that spiritual leaders hold attitudes toward and beliefs about money that color not only how they treat money but also their overall lifestyle and life choices. Spiritual leaders are not exempt from the cultural pressures that encourage people to live beyond their means. The truth is that spiritual leadership is rarely a lucrative proposition. No one goes into spiritual service for money. Unfortunately, some stay there for money (because they don't know what else to do to feed their family, even though they are miserable, leading them to feel trapped).

Suze Orman, well-known financial adviser, made it her practice to begin every new client interview with the same question: "What are you afraid of?" Her point is simple: beliefs power action, and fear is one of the primal motivators. This is Suze's way of helping her clients get in touch with what is driving their treatment of money. The issue is much larger than whether people have enough of it. People's attitudes toward money are often scripted from their family of origin, but they are unaware of the scripts they are acting out.

This was Claude's experience:

Every Saturday night at his boyhood home included a ritual meal of grilled steaks. Claude's dad grilled; Claude held the tray for the steaks and kept his dad company around the grill. This was a special time between the two, since Claude's dad often worked seven days a week and didn't have much time with him. Claude's father was a commissioned sales manager with a group of salespeople who reported their weekly sales to him each Saturday afternoon. So, guess what the conversation around the grill naturally included each week? Claude remembers that some weeks he wondered if they should be eating the steaks or putting them back in the freezer. Other weeks the steaks couldn't be big enough. That innocent weekly encounter taught Claude to worry about money. He is afraid there will never be enough. Even if there is now, there's always next week. He has never gone hungry or even seriously close to being without the money he needs. But it wasn't until Claude accessed this childhood ritual that he realized the source of his overall anxiety about money.

Other scripts about money that can become problems involve compulsive spending. Some people spend money to make themselves feel good when they are down, or to reward themselves for something, or when they are happy. In other words, they use money to medicate their emotions. Some people go to the other extreme and live as compulsive savers. They have a hard time spending any money for fear it will run out. Others simply don't want to fool with money at all, so even when they have the money they procrastinate over paying bills, filing their taxes, or balancing their checkbooks.

Spiritual leaders have financial difficulties like everyone else. Not all of it results from their personal choices. Some encounter catastrophic health problems; still others have so little to begin with that any bump in the road (car trouble, for instance) creates a financial strain. The point to this discussion is to highlight how important it is not to mismanage this part of life in a way that would jeopardize your ability to lead—and to be a great leader. Steve, whose story started this section, recognized that he could not continue the way he had been going with money management. He took proactive steps to get him and his entire family into financial counseling. He made himself accountable to key people in his ministry. His bold and decisive action saved his leadership.

---

This chapter has identified some key areas of self-management: emotions, expectations, physical and mental vibrancy, temptations, emotional intelligence, and money. Chances are some feelings of discontentment have been stirred up in you, because, after all, you've gotten acquainted or reacquainted with some areas of your life that need better management. The question is: How do you respond to this? If you feel like you're a failure and are ready to throw in the towel and are frustrated that you've not "arrived," then discontentment is eating your lunch. If, on the other hand, you don't feel defeated by being challenged (since you figure everyone's dealing with some areas of their life that need attention), and you realize you will always have some work to do, then you are managing your discontentment.

Joseph comes to mind when thinking about a great spiritual leader who practiced self-management. This discipline did not develop all at once for him. His lording it over his brothers with his dream recitations of how they would bow down to him certainly didn't earn him any affection from them. This poor emotional intelligence on his part actually created such animosity toward him that his brothers sold him into slavery (after even considering killing him!). This traumatic episode apparently got Joseph's attention. From this low point he steadily climbed up. He refused to give in to a variety of temptations: self-importance, self-pity, inappropriate sexual relations, abuse of power, and revenge, just to name a few. Joseph's responses to his misfortunes of slavery and jail demonstrate a mastery of emotions and expectations. Rather than whine, he built relationships in prison that ultimately paved the way for his release. The discipline he brought to his governmental responsibilities allowed Egypt to prepare for famine. His success grew out of his own well-managed life. No one can characterize Joseph as anything but a great leader. Joseph's self-management played a key role in securing his legacy.

It will do the same for you.

# 3

# THE DISCIPLINE OF
# SELF-DEVELOPMENT

When Richard took over as lead pastor of a church that was in a decade-long slide, he applied everything he had learned about church growth to his new leadership assignment. The result was an amazing turnaround, as the church grew quickly and seemed to thrive. This result, paradoxically, brought Richard a new problem: success. He had built bigger facilities through the years to handle the church's growth, but now he was out of building options. So for the next few years he turned in desperation to every technique, program, and process he could find to try to maintain his weekly attendance numbers (Richard's score card).

With each passing year Richard grew more frustrated, burning out more staff and becoming more and more fearful that he wouldn't stay "at the top of his game" for the next ten years until he could retire. New ideas that challenged his program-centric, real-estate-bound church model made him angry and defensive. He'd rip apart the idea or discredit the practitioner or messenger so he wouldn't have to deal with the prospect of changing his ministry approach.

Bottom line: Richard is not going to make it. He will not finish well. His fears will all come to pass.

Greg has also enjoyed success. In a part of the country that doesn't grow big churches, he developed a regional megachurch that has been instrumental in introducing many people to faith in Jesus. At the twenty-fifth anniversary of the congregation, Greg came to an astonishing insight, which he later shared with his elder board and staff. "I realized," he explained to them, "that the approaches that caused us to be effective in the first twenty-five years would not help us be effective in the future." Even more bluntly he said, "The younger generations don't care about all the ways we measure our success." He has launched the congregation into a three-year process, designed to change the church's score-card to reflect the emergence of the missional church.

Greg has made a decision to grow, to stretch, to change—to develop! He is positioning himself to finish well. Now in his late fifties, he is choosing the path of continued self-development.

Great leaders never stop developing. Moses picked up a whole new set of skills at age forty, then assumed his major leadership role forty years after that. Abraham became a world traveler at seventy, then a father two decades later. Paul went to the desert to get his head on straight after his Damascus road experience—an event that caused him to rethink his theology and his life mission. The apostle didn't begin his missionary journeys until his forties.

Two key practices show up commonly in great leaders who adopt the discipline of self-development as a life habit. They pursue lifelong learning, and they build on their strengths. In our discussion we give attention to both of these self-improvement practices. Then we examine how leaders develop failure-tolerance. The reason for this is simple: *every leader experiences failure at some level.* Great leaders, however, refuse to accept failure as a destination. They recast failure into an opportunity for self-development.

## Lifelong Learning

When I first met Mike, he seemed a fairly run-of-the-mill guy. His introduction of himself to the group of leaders sounded just like everyone else's. But only minutes into a personal conversation, that initial perception was obliterated. "I came alive when I turned sixty," he told me, with a twinkle in his eye and a half-grin on his face. "I'm not sure what I was doing before then." Now he is reading two books a week in every field from quantum physics to psychology to science fiction. He has been attending conferences addressing various aspects of leadership, and he is paying attention to what's going on in the world around him and in his community.

"Coming alive" for Mike also meant entering pastoral ministry and planting a new church. His ministry targets people struggling with drug addiction, broken families, and economic challenges. His congregation feeds hundreds of people every week.

I met Mike, not surprisingly, at a leadership learning experience designed primarily for young leaders. Truthfully, he is one of the youngest leaders I have ever met, despite his chronological age. What is Mike's secret? He says, "I've had to change my thinking through the years." Easier said than done, apparently, given the number of leaders I have been around who have not had a new thought in years.

## The Unlearning Curve

Lifelong learning actually means lifelong *unlearning*. Mike's capacity to grow through the years rested on his willingness to put yesterday's ideas, attitudes, and approaches under the knife of new insights and new challenges. The unlearning curve often proves steeper than the learning curve.

Just ask the apostle Paul. When the Pharisee realized that the messianic kingdom had already been ushered in (something Pharisees thought would occur at the end of time), inaugurated by the resurrection of a man condemned as unrighteous (only the righteous were to be raised), he was confronted by a scenario that challenged his theological construct. Not only did he realize he had been mistakenly fighting the Messiah of God (thinking he was defending the faith), he had to figure out how to reconcile the radical monotheism of his Hebrew understanding of God with the reality of Incarnation. No wonder he had to go into the desert. His three-day period of blindness riveted his attention on the last thing he saw: the resurrected Jesus. Everything in him had to come to grips with this new reality. Fortunately for us, Paul was willing to travel the unlearning curve.

The fields of unlearning range across a wide spectrum of issues that include the following:

• *Psychological insights that leaders need to have about themselves and others.* What emotional issues threaten to derail the leader? What types of acquaintances and associations limit instead of enhance the leader's ability?

• *Ministry methodologies.* What ministry approaches are no longer effective? How does technology create ministry opportunities? How can resources be refocused for a missional church expression?

• *The skill of cultural exegesis.* This skill has become a critical one in spiritual leaders' portfolios. The world at the beginning of the third millennium bears much closer resemblance to A.D. 30 than it does to 1970. This means leaders must reexamine their worldview.

The church is having to play catch-up to the Spirit again, just as it did in the book of Acts. The Kingdom Age is fast eclipsing the dominant Church culture. The Christian movement is again taking to the streets, to the marketplace, to homes, moving out of institutional settings and beyond institutional control. Spiritual leaders who have trained for institutional leadership, who anchor their leadership in positional authority, and who rely on educational credentialing don't understand the new expectations for leadership rooted in personal credibility, legitimized by followers, not external agencies. Leaders locked in the old world still believe that people think in secular-versus-sacred dichotomies and are expressing their spiritual quest by looking for a great church to join. Only unlearning those tried-and-true assumptions and practices will equip leaders to move with and meet these new conditions.

Leaders who refuse to engage in lifelong unlearning set themselves up to be relics of a world that is fast passing away (except where it is preserved in self-contained religious clubs). They run the risk of not only missing greatness but of sliding into ineffectiveness, as they and their organizations become irrelevant. They stunt their growth. They die in place, even if they don't get "buried" for several more years.

## Lifelong Learning Practices

Lifelong learning takes many forms, depending on the leader's cognitive style. Some leaders go inside themselves when they process information, preferring reading, writing, and reflecting as ways to figure out what they think or to take in new material they need in order to move forward. Others come to their conclusions externally, some not knowing what they think until they hear themselves or others say it. Their learning experiences almost always involve others through discussion and dialogue, even debate.

Some leaders pursue academic study, either in their original field or another; others attend seminars and conferences. Some leaders take up new hobbies or sports. Many leaders take on new leadership challenges or assignments as paths for learning. This approach forces the leader into accountability for growth. For some, the academic track provides this kind of accountability.

Regardless of style, however, all leaders who engage in lifelong learning evidence two characteristics. First, they are intentional about it. Their learning and self-development are not haphazard or random. Their path is not necessarily designed with a destination in mind (like a terminal degree), but they know what they want to explore and have a strategy to get there.

Second, these leaders' learning journeys are designed to expose them to new ideas. They are curious. They want to look at new vistas. They want new conversations. They devise new learning opportunities. Seeking out new ideas can be as simple as reading in a new subject or a new author or making the acquaintance of a new colleague, community leader, or thinker. Many leaders who are determined to understand the emerging world, for instance, are hanging out with teenagers and young college students. These young people are the guides into the new world for those of us who arrived on the planet during the last Ice Age.

## Learning Networks

Increasing numbers of lifelong learner-leaders have either created or joined intentional learning networks. These networks are organic and fluid, based in shared affinities such as a worldview-ministry paradigm and a similar ministry assignment (church leader, staff member, and so on). Some ministry associations provide a learning network for their members as part of the value-added features of membership. Some denominations facilitate the emergence of these networks (learning communities or learning clusters) by providing resources, recruiting facilitators, and convening the networks. Some seminaries promote this approach to learning in their curriculum process (by creating learning cohorts). Leadership Network serves as an example of a para-church agency that sponsors learning communities around various ministry challenges. Other learning communities are just springing up, as leaders create them for themselves as part of their own personal development.

Generational characteristics tend to play out in the way these networks organize and function. Boomers tend to prefer a small-group network of peer-practitioners who get together and drive their own learning with a clear learning agenda. Gen-X leaders are more open to a mentor-convener who generally opens up lives and hearts for examination and download. For them, learning is more relational. They usually approach a mentor with the request just to hang out with them. Barnes & Noble or Starbucks is a classroom of choice with this crowd.

Several reasons account for the rise of learning networks. First, smart leaders realize the short shelf life of whatever formal preparation they had for their role. They are aware that a new world poses new leadership challenges across the board, from shifting paradigms to enhancing skills to developing resources to nurturing personal development. Leaders can no longer adequately build knowledge alone; there is simply too much to learn. Privatized learning not only fails in its ability to deliver adequate content; its process is also fundamentally flawed. Collegial learning allows leaders to check their own biases and prejudices, to question their assumptions, to figure out what they don't see that keeps them from learning.

Another factor pushing the development of the learning community is the ascendancy of relational learning in the postmodern world. Intriguingly, this development actually goes back to the way education was done in the premodern world, when teachers and pupils were much more closely bound together in a learning relationship. The mass standardization of the modern era (courtesy of the advent of the printing press) shifted the emphasis in education to curriculum, with didactic instruction that supplemented textbooks. The teacher became central as the disseminator of information, the expert passing on knowledge to those who did not have it. In relational learning the learners help to drive the process by framing the learning agenda (based on the learners' challenges) and by taking responsibility for learning outcomes. The relationship between mentor and learner sets the "load limit" of information that can be exchanged and the speed limit of how fast knowledge can be developed. If significant trust and authenticity characterizes the relationship, then a broad range of issues can be more easily addressed and at a quicker pace.

Finally, the rise of learning networks acknowledges the recent trend of leaders who enter spiritual leadership roles from other careers. These leaders are less likely than their predecessors to put their call on hold for years to go through academic course work and credentialing before engaging in active leadership. These leaders, coming from business and educational backgrounds, are often highly competent and usually highly motivated people who feel a sense of urgency to shift their life work, so they are anxious to be deployed and engaged as rapidly as possible. These leaders bring a boatload of skill and experience to the table. They just want to get with other leader-practitioners to shorten their learning curve and to accelerate their development so they can take on and succeed in their current assignment.

Biblical precedent certainly exists for this approach to learning. With the whole world to save, Jesus created a learning community. That band of disciple-learners took on the stewardship of the move-ment. Jesus' method of preparation was to send them out (before they were ready!) and debrief their experiences. He let them observe him at work and debriefed their observations. He allowed them to listen to his teaching and debriefed their learning. He promised them a learning environment that would be even better after he left. By the time the Spirit came, the disciples had learned to debrief their lives and their experiences. That was what was going on in the upper room between Ascension and Pentecost. That's what went on in the aftermath of the Samaritan and Gentile Pentecosts (Acts 8 and 10). That is still the central activity of learning networks: debriefing the spiritual leader's life and ministry.

The way learning networks look is as varied as the personality and experience of the leader. But you can be certain of this: find a great leader, and you will find a commitment to lifelong learning as a core value. You will also find a cadre of learners around that leader.

## Building on Strengths

Great leaders differ from good leaders, in part, because of the degree to which they have developed and built on their strengths. These leaders have figured out that their best shot at making their great-est contribution to the world is for them to get better at what they are already good at. So they have decided to focus on their talent—identifying it and developing it.

Making this determination has been counterintuitive because building on our strengths is not what our culture teaches us. Our culture focuses on weaknesses, not on strengths. Just let a student come home from school with a report card bearing four A's and one C. What do you think the discussion will be about? Or imagine many conversations with kids who show talent in one area, only to be directed to spend their time and energy working in another area where they do not show as much potential—all in an effort to "balance them out." Here's a newsflash: people are not balanced! God did not design or build us to be balanced. Our talent, our passions, our personalities are all ways we are "out of round," where we are not "normal" or "average."

The result of our culture's obsession with weakness is that each of us is very well acquainted with what we are not good at. We can all recall some comments by coaches, teachers, parents, and peers who pointed out our lack of talent in this area or that. Unfortunately, many leaders spend all their lives trying to prove to someone they can overcome their weaknesses instead of capitalizing on their strengths. I once ran into a worship team leader who couldn't sing but was determined to prove everyone wrong who told him that. His determination that he be "used by God"—untalented as he was—missed the biblical teaching that we are stewards of the talent we have, not the talent we don't have or simply wish we had.

Although most of us can easily rattle off a list of the things we don't do well, many leaders cannot identify what they are truly good at. Said another way, many of us are naïve about our talent. Ted Williams, the legendary baseball hitter, was once asked to help coach a rookie who had just arrived from the minors. Williams stood at the batting cage and watched the newbie fan at a few 95-miles-per-hour fastballs.

"Hey kid," the pro called out. "Just watch the stitches."

"Huh?" the kid replied.

"Just watch the stitches," Williams repeated.

"What stitches?" the rookie asked, bewildered.

"On the baseball!" Williams exclaimed, and then proceeded to give a detailed description of how the rotation of the stitches influenced how the ball behaves between the pitching mound and home plate.

"You can see stitches?" the rookie asked incredulously.

Commenting on that story, other players say that a 95-miles-per-hour fastball coming in from the mound to the plate is a blur the first 10 feet after it leaves the pitcher's hand; for the other 50'6" it is invisible! Yet Ted Williams was serious about his advice to "watch the stitches." Why would he give that young ball player such bad advice? Because he thought everyone could see stitches. He was not even aware of his talent. His teammates asked him what else he could see on the baseball. He replied, "On a good day I can read the commissioner's signature."

Every leader can easily and readily "see the stitches" in the area where he or she has been gifted. This truth challenges another common myth that "it only counts if it comes hard." In the area of our talent, ability comes easy. Seeing stitches didn't come hard for Ted Williams. Our culture teaches us to devalue what comes easy, so we fail to have an honest assessment of what we are good at.

Talent matters. The sooner we figure this out, the sooner we can cooperate with God in figuring out our best contribution. Otherwise, we are doomed to mediocrity at best or to repeated failure at worst. Although we have been told and encouraged that if we dream it, if we believe it, we can achieve it, that's not true. I could wish to be an NBA guard all day long. I could go to NBA guard camp, be mentored by an NBA guard, and join an NBA guard learning cluster. It wouldn't matter. I will never be an NBA guard. I don't have the talent. Talent counts—both the talent we have and the talent we don't. Great leaders have an honest assessment of both.

## Becoming Aware of Strengths

During his lifetime Donald Clifton, former CEO and chairman of the board of The Gallup Organization, crusaded to help people discover and build on their talent. He passionately contended that people are more fulfilled when they are working from their strengths. He observed that people had fairly complete vocabularies for weaknesses, thanks to our culture. Even though we may not have any medical training or background in psychology, we are fairly well acquainted with neuroses and various psychological conditions like depression, bipolar disorder, attention deficit disorder, various syndromes, paranoia, and schizophrenia. Yet, Clifton noticed, we have no corresponding language for strengths. Part of his legacy was the development of the Gallup StrengthsFinder—an instrument that helps people identify their top talents and provides a taxonomy that helps users explore their own and others' talent. (For further exploration of the Gallup StrengthsFinder, pick up a copy of *Now, Discover Your Strengths* by Marcus Buckingham and Donald O. Clifton.[5])

Clifton and others have suggested that people can gain strengths awareness, even without the help of a research instrument, if they pay attention to a few key indicators.

**A *Sense of Accomplishment*.**  In the movie *Chariots of Fire*, one scene involves a conversation between the Scottish Olympic runner Eric Liddell and his sister Jennie. Liddell attempts to explain to her why he is postponing his missionary deployment to run in the Olympics. "God made me for a purpose—China. But he also made me fast. When I run I feel his pleasure." That sense of feeling the smile of God, the wind in your sails, that sense of privilege to get to do something, the feeling that you are doing what you were born to do—these are the tell-tale signs of talent, of personal strengths. What is it that you feel most fully alive doing?

***Glimpses of Excellence*.**  Real talent shows off; it can't help it. Even if you don't intend it or don't value talent yourself, others will notice. The key here is not to look for full-blown excellence (though that might be present) but for glimpses or sparks that point to underdeveloped talent. For example, a teacher pointed out to Luke, a would-be engineering student, that he had a knack for writing. This simple comment led to a redirection for Luke that took him into a much more fulfilling career. As he looks back, he realizes how miserable he would have been had he not paid attention to this gift but instead followed his plan to enter his dad's engineering consulting practice. "Seeing stitches" (or whatever form your talent takes that compares with Ted Williams's talent) sets you apart from the rest of the pack. Practicing this talent is your most effective strategy for making your best contribution.

**Quick Learning.**    In the area of your talent, you learn quickly. God wired you for rapid learning, for quickly grasping what you need to excel in this area. In areas where you are not talented, you struggle more. I remember coaching my oldest daughter to drop back one level in her math classes in high school when it became apparent that math was not going to be something she enjoyed or learned very rapidly. This decision would take her out of the honors track in that subject area. With her high sense of responsibility, she felt she should trudge on. At one point in my life I would have said something like, "You started this track; you're going to finish it," or something similarly stupid. But because I had come to a conviction about building on strengths, I told my daughter that if she stayed in her current math level, it was going to consume all her energy and soak up time from other studies that really jazzed her and promised to help her discover her true strengths and interests. The character of her whole semester shifted for the better with that decision. She recaptured hours she could spend on activities and school subjects that she enjoyed. The fog of failure lifted, helping to brighten her attitude—a benefit that spilled into every area of her life.

**Sustained Growth.**    In our areas of talent, we are both willing to grow and capable of continued development. We do not tire of using our talent. This is why professional athletes paid millions of dollars still show up for practice and hire personal trainers and coaches to help them get even better. I believe we will carry our talent into eternity. (Since the Bible clearly teaches that our personalities and ethnicities remain intact in heaven, why not the talent we have been given?) I suspect there are uses for our talent that we have not yet imagined. We are practicing for eternity when we practice our talent.

**Feedback.**    Other people can be a tremendous source of affirmation and confirmation if we can solicit good feedback from them and if we do not demur too quickly when people begin telling us what we do well. Spiritual leaders all too often obsess over negative feedback and blow off positive information. Invite people to tell you what you do well. Probe behind their compliments and observations. Ask them, "What about my performance is most helpful, or excellent, or praiseworthy? How does this talent show up? Can you describe how my performance in this area comes across and the impact it makes on others?" These and other questions can give you valuable coaching tips on how to continue your strength development.

One of the dilemmas I find among spiritual leaders is a propensity to downplay positive feedback and focus on negative feedback. This is a recipe for continued mediocrity because it pegs your productivity to problems and demoralizes you to boot. Remember, it is okay for you not to be good at everything. That qualifies you for being human. Being human is what qualifies you for spiritual leadership, not being perfect. The need to be good at everything is idolatrous. Besides, not getting all the talent is one more way God builds into us our need for community. We need other people's talent to fully experience what God has in mind for our lives.

## Developing a Strengths Culture

As a leader you have major responsibility for shaping the culture of your ministry and organization. So why not be good to yourself and others through developing a culture that values and cultivates the strengths of everyone who is part of it? This practice will buck the usual approach in organizational and church life, where people are hired for what they are good at, then beaten up for what they don't do well. This dynamic shows up at the volunteer level when we recruit people for their ability, then proceed to evaluate them on the basis of their shortcomings. But it doesn't stop there; the switcheroo extends to the level of paid leaders. Many congregations, for instance, when looking for new leadership, call the new pastor to fix the last pastor! Then, to top it off, they discover they like the previous pastor more than they thought! Guess who pays for this discovery?

Strengths-conscious leaders not only ask, "What should be done?" But they should also ask, "Based on talent, who should have this assignment?" When professional football coaches decide to kick a field goal, they call in their field goal kicker. How absurd would it be to give that assignment to someone who just wants to be a kicker, or as a way to get a player involved in the game, or even to pull in a fan who is a major donor to give him a moment in the spotlight? How demoralizing would that be to the rest of the team? How many games would that coach win? Why would talent hang around this kind of situation? As crazy as this sounds, much of the whining I hear from leaders about not having adequate talent, or not enjoying winning seasons—or whatever—is directly related to poor talent management.

None of this discussion of building on strengths is intended to ignore weaknesses. Obviously, you have to address the ways that keep your people and organization from moving ahead. The key is in how you do it. If your approach involves focusing on people's weaknesses, you will foster an underperforming culture.

I often tell the story of Frank, the mythological (but all-too-real!) car salesman who knocked the ball out of the park every month in sales but struggled with his paperwork. So the dealership shipped him off to paperwork school, where he had his nose rubbed in his poor performance. Nevertheless, Frank is a high achiever and throws himself into a new commitment to doing quality paperwork. However, because it takes so much energy and time for Frank to do his paperwork, guess what happens to his sales? Eventually, Frank gets to the point where he thinks, "If I sell another car it will kill me!" By focusing on Frank's weakness, we have obliterated his talent and quenched his enthusiasm for what he does superbly well. Sound familiar?

Better ways of managing performance weakness include recruiting others who have the talent you need, reassigning work responsibilities to match talent, and outsourcing to talent outside the organization. I have been intrigued to see that some congregations are using video venues that feature a superb communicator from elsewhere for teaching, which frees the local pastoral staff to focus on other strengths.

Developing a strengths-based culture also involves giving people permission to quit doing things they are not good at. This will mean strategizing on how to accomplish these tasks or figuring out whether these functions need to be done at all. We do not do people any favors by getting them into situations that don't match their talent. Others wind up getting frustrated with them or even losing respect for their other abilities. One ministry organization, in response to a vacancy on its executive team level, called in one of its most respected ministers to fill the role. Unfortunately, the talent match didn't work. The skills that made the minister effective in local situations were not the talents needed for office administration. The tragedy of the situation is not that the assignment didn't work out but that people throughout the ministry organization lost respect for a formerly highly regarded person—a loss that was totally unnecessary had the minister's strengths been recognized and honored.

Spiritual leaders need to ward off an insidious perfectionism that may permeate their thinking. Carrying unrealistic expectations about your own and others' performance eventually violates people by robbing them of the joy of celebrating their strengths. It is idolatrous as well to set aside God's work in people through his sovereign distribution of talent and substitute another design requirement that is fabricated around organizational requirements, not people development. God is in the people-development enterprise. He didn't plant a garden and then decide to create people to take care of it. The chores in Paradise were designed to help Adam grow. This dynamic became confused after the Fall. God predicted to Adam that as a result of sin's entrance into the world, work would become frustrating rather than fulfilling. As a spiritual leader, your commitment to building a strengths-based culture helps to lift the curse.

## Avoiding Burnout

Our strengths are also our needs. Said another way, we each need to do what we do well. If we don't get a chance to perform in the area of our talents, we feel cheated, grow frustrated, and court burnout.

Most ministry burnout among spiritual leaders is not the exotic type (usually involving some egregious moral failure) that garners all the press and gossip. Instead, it is typically the common garden variety of burnout that results from leaders dealing day in and day out with stuff that brings them no energy and does not play to their talents. Eventually, leaders run out of emotional, psychological, and spiritual reserve. A strong sense of call or commitment or a highly developed sense of responsibility may keep the leader in place, but only a shell of the formerly vibrant person remains. This happens far too frequently in spiritual leadership circles to be ignored. Moving toward areas of strength, including talent and passions, provides one clear strategy for avoiding burnout.

Leaders who choose greatness decide to become better at what they are good at. They strategize as to how they can do more of what brings them energy. They develop strengths-based cultures and flee toxic environments that threaten to suck the life out of them by chaining them to areas for which they have neither passion nor talent.

## Developing Through Failure

Although no one wants to get really good at failure, leaders need to learn to deal with the inevitable. Some failures seek you out; others are self-manufactured. All failures present the leader with choices of how to deal with the failure. Whether to shrink or to grow. Whether to learn or to derail.

When a leader fails, certain practices compound the failure: blaming, hiding, recriminating, excusing, diverting, to name a few. The negative impact of these approaches needs little amplification. All of us are tempted to take the low road when we fail. It is a natural survival instinct to want to off-load the failure to someone or something else. But it doesn't work.

Great leaders accept failure but don't let it be "the book" on them. They adopt some very important practices and approaches to their failures.

***Admit the Mistake.*** The first practice may be the hardest. Admitting mistakes is a character test, with the test getting harder with each added layer of responsibility and level of leadership influence. When the stakes are high, admitting mistakes is hard. Saying "I've made a mistake" is only a start. The key is to be specific. What, exactly, was the mistake? Was it poor moral choices? Was it failure to pay attention to something? Whatever it was, name it.

One leader admitted to her constituents that she had developed some poor work and life habits that had diminished her leadership effectiveness. She specifically detailed an overcrowded schedule, a failure to take adequate rest, and the resulting impairment of judgment in some key decisions that had proved costly. It was a gutsy move, rewarded not only with a strong affirmation of support by her followers but also by the large number of people who came forward to discuss their own similar life choices and mismanagement so they could get some help. Organizational health improved dramatically as a result of a profound honesty on the leader's part.

*Accept Responsibility.* Business consultant Jim Collins describes what he calls Level 5 leadership. Few leaders attain this level—the best in the leadership-development chain. Level 5 leaders, Collins observes, use both windows and mirrors. When things are going well, they point out to all the people beyond them who make it possible. When things don't go well, these same leaders stand in front of the mirror and take responsibility for the failure.

On February 9, 2001, navy commander Scott Waddle gave an order to perform an emergency maneuver that inadvertently caused the nuclear submarine he commanded to rapidly rise up through the water to the surface. There it smashed into the Ehime Maru, a Japanese fishing boat. As a result of the collision, nine people died. Against legal advice, Commander Waddle took the witness stand and assumed responsibility for the actions of his crew that led to the tragedy. This took enormous courage, in light of a litigious culture that often leads people to disavow responsibility for fear of being sued.

*Make Restitution.* Sometimes saying "I'm sorry" is not enough. Have people been hurt? Have people sustained losses that the leader can address? What can be done privately? What must be done publicly? The leader who triumphs over failure moves quickly to acts of restitution.

Zaccheus's pledge to repay and overpay those from whom he had extorted money in his role as tax collector instructs us in this practice. It wasn't enough that Zaccheus got right with God. His conversion came with some getting-right-with-people business attached to it. His acts of restitution did not save him, but they proved the authenticity of his conversion experience and the seriousness of his new faith.

**_Reassess Life Vision and Values._**  In the face of failure, the leader must take an interior journey to reassess what he or she is doing and why. Often the failure threatens to derail the leader's life mission. It can cloud the leader's vision of what he wants to accomplish and believes he can do. The leader often needs to return to God's life call for soul nourishment. This is what Moses did when initial attempts at Exodus proved futile, and he was humiliated in front of his kinsmen.

Leaders also need to evaluate their values as part of facing failure. Often failed values account for the failure itself: integrity may have been compromised; relationships may have been damaged. The attention to values will bring the leader back to center. Some repair work may be needed. Followers may need reassurance that the leader has returned to core values. The leader must expect to have to win back confidence if people feel betrayed.

Marvin's accomplishments, simply put, had gone to his head. The result was not pretty. He had moved from being a servant to having expectations of being served. Staff members who previously were treated as valued coworkers were now subject to his unrealistic expectations, as well as demeaning outbursts of temper and ridicule. An intervention by the ministry board served Marvin the wake-up call he needed. Though Marvin was repentant, it took several months to convince his coworkers of his genuine recommitment to them.

***Mourn Your Loss.*** Failure involves loss. The losses may include relationships, credibility, leadership influence, self-esteem, or sense of direction. You will not be able to fully overcome the failure until you deal with the loss. Recovery relies on grieving fully.

Grieving as a leader is risky business. When David grieved Absalom, his grief was viewed by his second-in-command as inappropriate, given the fact that other lives were on the line. David had to tuck his grief away for private expression. On the other hand, sometimes it is appropriate for the leader to acknowledge publicly the loss and grief that failure has precipitated. Ronald Reagan's handling of the *Challenger* explosion is a classic lesson in this leadership requirement. His obvious sense of grief helped a nation mourn its loss. Although people need hope and confidence from their leader, they will not follow a leader whom they feel is not genuine.

Let those you trust help you mourn. This will honor them and their relationship to you. Not to turn to your confidants at this point is unhealthy. To retreat to a shell is not good. To refuse help because you just want to "deal with it" by yourself will deny the power of healing in community.

***Move to Closure.*** Leaders don't have the luxury of wallowing around in their grief. This is another reason it is good for leaders to involve confidants who can move them along through the grief process. Although the leader must put the loss behind as quickly as possible, it is important to let others take the time they need. Leaders who demand that everyone "get over it" come across as callous and uncaring. The move to closure on the leader's part gives him or her the focus to attend to other leadership demands (which may, in fact, include helping others grieve). Followers need the confidence that the leader is on the job, not mired down by one episode of failure.

***Accept Direction.*** The level of guidance a leader needs depends on the failure. If the failure is personal, the leader will need extraordinary people who can show him the loving grace of God. If the failure is a poor decision in leadership, then the guidance will need to be of a different sort. Nevertheless, times of failure are times to submit to trusted others and mentors for debriefing and for learning. The decision to submit to others at this point is a critical choice to move toward greatness.

As a young spiritual leader, I was privileged to meet with a well-known Christian leader whose moral failure had cost him his ministerial position. He recounted his decision to put himself under the direction of three other people who knew him well and could be trusted to tell him the truth. Based on their counsel, he took some time off to deal with personal and family issues. When he reentered spiritual leadership, he was much more self-aware and was emotionally and spiritually healthier.

**Establish New Behaviors and Accountabilities.**  Behaviors and decision-making processes that contributed to the failure need to be changed—quickly. Appropriate accountabilities need to be instituted. One pastor who admitted to struggles with pornography made himself accountable to a group of pastor friends whom he empowered to check on him. Another leader misused some money in a discretionary account for personal emergency needs. His financial board established new accounting procedures. A church board rewrote their covenant of how they would handle personnel failures after they handled a staff firing poorly.

Failure is inevitable, whether small or large. Use the checklist given here to make sure you grow through your failure personally and become even more useful to God and developed in your leadership role in the kingdom.

---

Mark Twain once said of an acquaintance who had passed away: "He died at thirty; they buried him at sixty." Don't die in place! Keep learning, focus on your strengths, and grow through failure. Practicing these habits of self-development will help qualify your leadership for greatness.

# 4

# THE DISCIPLINE
# OF MISSION

"I have resigned my current position," Jessica related to me over the phone. "I'm sending you my résumé. If you think of some place that needs a small-group pastor, feel free to share it with them." Then, after a sigh, she said, "Though I'm not sure I want to do the same thing, just in another place."

That was my cue. "Why don't you send me four or five sentences that tell me what you'd really like to do?" I said. "Also, tell me what kind of environment would support the ministry you envision."

"Sure, I can do that." Jessica replied. "You'll have it next week."

Weeks went by. Finally, I heard from her. "These are the hardest two paragraphs I've ever written," she wrote in the opening lines of the e-mail to introduce what followed. When I read what she had written, I could understand why she felt that way. In our initial conversation Jessica had been looking for a job. Her e-mail convinced me she was now a woman on a mission.

The process of sorting through what she really wanted to do next changed Jessica's life. She realized that not only did she *not* want a church job similar to the last; she didn't want to work in a church at all. Her real interest, she discovered, was establishing a community ministry that connects with people through recreational activity. Jessica's mission will take her outside the institutional church setting into the streets with the gospel. She has become completely jazzed by the possibilities for the future—a far cry from that tired woman who had called me weeks earlier.

Not every leader I similarly challenge responds like Jessica. Mitchell poured out his frustration over lunch. His current place of leadership service was bringing him no joy. In fact, he told me, it was slowly killing him. "Why don't you do something different?" I asked. "You are obviously miserable and the prospects for things improving are practically nil." Based on my five years of experience with Mitch, I pressed on. "Besides, you're not particularly suited for the role you are in. So even if you go somewhere else that is better but take on the same role, you're still going to be miserable in the long run."

"You're right," Mitch admitted. "But I can't afford to quit. Besides, I don't know what else to do." Even though we explored several options for Mitch's life—all more in line with his talents and his interests—he chose to remain in a work environment that frustrates him rather than figure out a way to reorient his life around a core mission.

People, even leaders, typically define themselves in terms of jobs, position descriptions, roles. When asked what they are about in life, they respond with, "I'm a _____ (fill in the blank with some line of work)" or "I work at _____ (some company or organization)."

Great leaders, on the other hand, tell you what they are intending to accomplish, the mission they are on. "I am working to change _____" or "I am investing my life in _____ in order to _____." These leaders speak in terms of contribution, of significance, of changing the world. They don't work for an organization; the organization works for them. Their job, their role, their current assignment is the venue or platform from which they pursue their life mission. No matter what job they take or role they fill, they redefine the position to fit their mission, not the other way around. They do not hammer their mission into fitting their work assignment. Just the opposite is true. The life mission of great leaders determines the content of their days, of their work, of their energies and talents. In short, great leaders practice the discipline of mission.

## Jesus and Mission

Early in Jesus' public ministry he tipped his hand on his mission and its power to order his life, especially how he went about ministering and teaching to people.

> Very early in the morning, while it was still dark, Jesus got up, left the house and went off to a solitary place, where he prayed. Simon and his companions went to look for him, and when they found him, they exclaimed: "Everyone is looking for you!" Jesus replied, "Let us go somewhere else—to the nearby villages—so I can preach there also. *That is why I have come*" [emphasis added; Mark 1:35–38, NIV].

Did you catch that? Did Jesus not understand the Messiah job? Didn't he know that he was supposed to be available to people, to meet their needs, to help them? Here they were crying out for him, desperate for him, and he decided to turn away from them! What drove him to that decision? Simply put, Jesus knew why he was on the planet. His mission was to get the word out throughout that region, not set up camp in one spot. There were plenty of people who needed healing in every town. But the need was not the call. Jesus was not about to put the mission at risk, even as drawn to people and their needs as he was. He shocked his disciples and disappointed some followers, but he maintained missional integrity. Jesus' sense of mission enabled him to know what to say no to so he could say yes to the reason he had come to earth.

I have been around countless numbers of spiritual leaders who are dying to hear, "Everyone is looking for you." Their personal sense of worth is determined by their being sought after or needed. So they give away their vitality and missional direction to whomever or whatever the need of the hour is or the latest crisis (sometimes a crisis they themselves generated!).

Great leaders have not escaped these temptations. They do not lack for opportunities. But they do not chase every one. Nor are they sheltered from people's needs. But they understand that the need is not necessarily the call for them to engage it. They do not lack challenges. But they know they don't have to fight every fight or take every cause. Great leaders pick the causes, seize the opportunities, and address the needs that fall in line with their mission.

## Discovering Your Mission

Great spiritual leaders understand that their mission is not something they invent. Rather, they realize that their life mission is something they discover. They believe God is the One who has determined their life assignment. He has gone to great efforts at sowing clues in the leader's life to help foster this discovery process. Talent, passion, experiences, successes, personality traits, opportunities—all provide helpful hints in this discovery process. Great leaders discern a divine pattern for an intentional path to significance and fulfillment. These gifts and clues are interrelated. Together they form a picture of the leader's mission—the one that guides his life's efforts, much the way an image on the box lid of a jigsaw puzzle helps the puzzle worker know what to look for and see how the pieces of the puzzle fit together.

### Call

Spiritual leaders often refer to their "call" as a synonym for what is being described here as "mission." Because they may or may not be the same, this can be confusing. Too many spiritual leaders have locked their call into one particular way of being expressed or pursued. For instance, "I am called to be a pastor," is a phrase I hear frequently when leaders are discussing with me their next chapter of life. Then they often proceed to tell me exactly what kind of church they feel called to and where they want it to be located. I don't easily question a sense of God's call on their life, but reducing it to a preferred place of employment and a particular job description seems somehow to reduce the spiritual depth of genuine call.

What happens to someone's sense of call when a congregational position doesn't open up? Or one doesn't open up that can pay the bills? Even worse, what happens to a leader's view of God in this case? Was God capricious with his call? Why would he call and not provide a place of service? I have seen too many leaders on the ropes financially and spiritually due to a shallow understanding of call. They don't know what else to do if God doesn't provide them a way of "doing ministry" that fits their template.

Feeling the call "to pastor" or "to the ministry" is different from feeling a call "to be a pastor." The call to pastor contains a spiritual dynamism that transcends a vocational career path. Pastoring is a call that can be expressed in many ways,—from leading local congregations to serving as a pastoral counselor to chaplaining military personnel or prison inmates to leading a house church to pastoring pastors. This pastoring may either be paid or volunteer; it may be a career or a bivocational pursuit. The leader with this call is expressing a life mission that is oriented around and arising out of his or her person. How it gets expressed may change over time or depending on circumstances. The call does not hinge on having the title of "pastor" or drawing a salary from a local congregation. As I've said, the venue provides a platform for the leader to purse a life mission. The venue is negotiable; the mission is non-negotiable.

In my own case my life mission has remained the same since I was able to articulate it in my twenties: to work for the missional renewal of the North American church. I have pursued that mission in a variety of settings and platforms: twenty years in local congregational leadership, then through denominational leadership with my writing, consulting ministry organizations, coaching ministry practitioners, and teaching. Each venue has offered me an opportunity to push for missional renewal at the congregational and denominational levels, as well as with individual leaders for their personal lives and ministries. My mission has shaped the flavor of my leadership in each setting. One disgruntled man who left the church I was pastoring complained to another member, "Reggie only has nine sermons." At the time that comment bruised me (since I had been preaching there for ten years!). In retrospect, I think he was generous! The missional renewal theme is the song I sing, no matter the tune. This is the power of the leader's mission in terms of characterizing the content of his call.

The point to all of this is that I coach spiritual leaders to treat their call more fluently than most of them are inclined to do. They confuse the *content* of the call with the *context* of the call and how God might choose for them to live out the call in their lives. The need to be more flexible in this regard will be increasingly important for leaders as the expression of spirituality in North America moves beyond institutional settings into the street and marketplace. The desire to serve people in spiritual leadership will make the same transition. It already is. Each week I run into people who once pursued their call in the church but now are working in some aspect of community or business leadership as the way to express their call to ministry.

Spiritual leaders need to distill out the core, the essence, of their call from God. Some key questions might help provide some clues:

- What people or cause do you feel drawn to?
- What do you want to help people do or achieve or experience?
- How do you want to help people?
- What message do you want to deliver?
- How do you intend to serve or have an impact on the world?
- Why did you say yes to God to begin with?

Answers to these inquiries should help the leader understand more clearly his call and life mission.

Sid gave up his highly lucrative job in the building business to go to work at a church as an outreach pastor. He had a passion to reach young families who were unchurched. After a frustrating two years he reentered the business world, determined that the best way to fulfill his heart passion was outside church programming, right in the middle of doing business with customers. The church environment simply didn't feed his basic call: to intersect people in their daily lives with a life-transforming message. When Sid got in touch with the basic core of his call, he got over the confusion of where and how he was to live it out.

Monty's assessment of the essence of his call led him out of his pediatric practice into a local church ministry. He realized that he dreaded doing most of what went along with practicing medicine. What really motivated Monty were the relationships he developed in his clinic that opened up opportunities to coach people in their marital and family development. When he had distilled his thinking, he shut down his medical practice and moved on to a church staff as minister to families. The venue provides him with hours each week to follow his call now, rather than try to work his call in between patients' appointments in the course of a day.

## Passion

Another clue to a spiritual leader's life mission is passion, which can inform the arena where that leader's call is expressed or how it is focused. The leader's passion may be located around a particular group of people, for instance.

Mary loves young people, particularly high schoolers and young college students—kids in their mid-to-late teens. While other people have little patience with kids (for lots of reasons, ranging from their unpredictability to their musical tastes to their personal style preferences in hair color and body art), Mary has a heart for kids that communicates love and acceptance to them while also asking that they meet her high standards. She can dispense wisdom and advice without condescension. Mary is safe, and so is her home. She routinely hosts kids who hang out at her house or meets them out for coffee. The kids love her, because they know she loves them.

Mary would be one very unhappy camper if she were unable to pursue her mission. That's how leaders describe passion. It is emotional. Passion is what they can't live without; it's also what's worth dying for.

Unfortunately, many spiritual leaders refer to passion only in the past tense. They had it once, but somewhere along the way they lost it. Often a key to personal renewal for spiritual leaders is their getting back in touch with the passion of their soul and helping them chart a life path that gets them back to it or enables them to nurture their passion again. This path can often require that they make a courageous choice or set of choices. Their determination to reconnect with their passion may require a change in ministry location, in responsibility, in salary, maybe all three. If they stay in place, it usually demands they shift their calendar and ministry priorities—a decision that is not always popular with those they minister to and with.

> Aaron, a young pastor, came to our Joshua Project (our spiritual leadership "war college") at the very end of his rope spiritually and emotionally. As he talked about his leadership challenge, it became obvious that the setting where he was ministering not only did not line up with his strengths, it was toxic to his soul. He made a gutsy decision to begin a fresh dialogue with God about his life mission. Over the months that followed, Aaron got back in touch with his sense of call (what he said yes to when he entered ministry) and even began paying attention to a stirring in his heart for another country. He has since quit his paid ministry role and is working in a physically demanding marketplace position while pursuing his passion to move to another country to work with people whom he wants to reach with the gospel.

The sacrifice for Aaron in terms of position, pay, and prestige is enormous, but he is the happiest he has been in months. He would tell you the pursuit of his passion is worth it all.

Great spiritual leaders can articulate their passion. They know what makes their heart beat faster. They know what they do that enables them to feel the smile of God. They move toward their passion. They feed it. They are intentional and *alive*!

## Talent

Here it is again! Talent matters, in more ways than one! The subject of talent cropped up in our discussion of the leader's self-development. It also plays a huge part in providing a clue to the leader's life mission.

While every aspect of the earlier discussion on the leader's development of strengths doesn't need to be rehearsed, some of the major ideas are worth repeating. Your best shot at making your greatest contribution in the world is for you to get better at what you are already good at. Instead of focusing on weakness, focus on improving your strengths. Remember, your strengths are also your needs, meaning that you need to develop and use your talent in order to experience deep satisfaction at an emotional and spiritual level.

Unfortunately, many spiritual leaders do not make the connection between their talent and their life mission. God is not capricious. He does not give people certain talents and then send them out on a mission that doesn't fit their gifting. Because God has envisioned the leader's mission, he distributes talent accordingly. If more leaders understood this truth, fewer would labor under a false sense of humility. Many spiritual leaders speak often of how God has to work around them or in spite of their weaknesses. The truth is, God has not called you to your life mission *in spite of* who you are; he has called you precisely *because of* who you are.

The implications of this perspective prove significant in terms of talent and mission. If what a leader is engaged in doing does not play to his or her talent, then it needs to be realigned for better fit. If that is not feasible, the leader should devise an exit strategy for getting out. It's that simple. We make it more complicated than it needs to be because we don't take seriously the link between the creative handiwork of God and missional intentionality.

Some time back I had a struggle with my work assignments. I had assumed a level of responsibility in my denominational role that carried with it a lot of administration. Can I do administration? Yes. Is it the thing I live for? Assuredly not. Increasingly, I became aware that my life mission (the reason I was there) didn't match my organization performance agreement. My executive director helped me figure out a way to redesign my work to match my mission.

If you are not good at something, quit doing it, or at least do it as little as possible. If certain talents are prerequisites to having a particular ministry assignment and you don't have those talents, rethink whether you should perhaps give up that assignment to someone who does. Or you can assess whether the talent set is indeed critical to the effectiveness of a particular role or job. Perhaps those talents can be outsourced or reassigned. But all too often leaders trip up their own potential for greatness by staying in positions that require them to spend too much time on areas where they are weak, robbing time and energy from the talent that could significantly increase their leadership impact. And every time leaders insist on staying with work at which they are not talented, they prohibit someone else from being able to practice greatness by robbing them of the chance to practice their strengths.

Randy attended a continuing education conference for ministers that was sponsored by his denomination. As part of the experience he took an instrument that gave him insight into his preferred leadership style and ministry talent. As the group debriefed their discoveries, Randy found out that he had scored differently from other conference participants who had the same work assignments he did. A lightbulb went on for him. The others were energized and excited about their work. He was struggling with his role and assignments. Randy was frustrated and discouraged about doing the same things that were bringing the other members of his cohort great satisfaction. Randy suddenly realized that he was simply not fit for his staff position. There wasn't anything wrong with him; his strengths just didn't fit the role he had.

Randy's relief was palpable when he met his wife for lunch after the conference. He told her how he felt free to plan an exit strategy from a ministry assignment that was frustrating him. Had he stayed, determined to be "faithful" or "committed" or whatever rationale he would devise to support that decision, Randy would have been in danger of losing a key strategy for his personal development. Even more, he would probably have become toxic to the organization he was in because his frustration levels would eventually seep out and create confusion, toxicity, and blame.

Great leaders are separated from good leaders by the degree to which their personal strengths match with their life and ministry. Their mission is informed by what they bring to the table.

## Personality

Personality can also furnish a clue to the leader's mission. Are you more task-oriented, or do you draw energy from relational interactions? Do you prefer backstage assignments, or do you come alive in the spotlight? Do you prefer to think things through out loud with others in lively discussion, or do you prefer to get away by yourself to figure out what you think? While some leaders are worn out by a day at the office, some consider it a good day if they have not had a single interruption from their desk work. Some leaders enjoy leading from the 40,000-foot view, while others feel most alive when working one-on-one with people.

These and countless other personality qualities yield insights into the preferred environment for leaders. This is not to suggest that only one personality will work in any one given ministry assignment. Not only is that perspective too rigid; it is simply wrong. For instance, there have been great American presidents who were introverts (hardly the place you'd expect that personality to end up). However, these men were self-aware enough to protect themselves from the exhaustion of dealing with people.

The real issue is the leader's self-awareness about the fit between specific personality and spiritual leadership responsibilities. This often comes down to the issue of the culture of the leader's organization or ministry. I work with some leaders who are having trouble in their ministry because they simply don't enjoy a cultural "fit" with the organization or people they serve. The reasons for this are numerous, ranging from socioeconomic and psychographic factors to role expectations that don't mesh to a lack of shared values. Here are some examples of what I'm talking about.

> Gary doesn't understand that he is having trouble with his leadership style because he is employing authoritarian tactics in a college-town setting with a leadership board composed largely of academics.

> Shelby needs to be more assertive in his role working with blue-collar people, but his personality was shaped by a more collegial model.

> Sam has never figured out that he's not in rural Kansas anymore. His homespun lessons right off the farm have limited appeal in his new suburban setting.

> Carla is swimming upstream against a club-member set of values in her attempt to move the church to be more missional. Eventually, either the club-member values or the missional values will prevail.

Each of these leaders, for various reasons, is struggling to "fit" their congregational culture.

I am not saying that God never pulls an intervention of the cross-cultural kind, nor am I suggesting that leaders serve only in places that are comfortable. We have examples of great leaders who never "fit in" (Moses comes to mind). Again, the issue is one of self-awareness about what kind of settings typically free leaders to be at their peak ability to exercise their mission and express their personality. Someone who is assigned to a place that militates against his or her personality will require very intentional nurture and self-maintenance in order to survive over time. God himself looked after Moses, spending more face time with him than any other leader in the Bible (except Jesus). He called Moses his friend and even took care of Moses' funeral arrangements.

More often than not, personality helps to shape the approach leaders take to their mission. Will you be an activist or philosopher? Will days start early, go late, or both? How will you motivate, challenge, and encourage? How will you cast vision? Who will you cultivate among other leaders? What kind of leadership culture will you develop? What style of decision making will you pursue?

The leader's personality also plays a significant role in shaping the composition of his or her leadership team. Others decide whether they want to or can be a participant in the leader's regime, often based on the leader's personality. Great leaders are stewards of their own personality. They know who it attracts and who will be repelled by it. They know when to dial it up and when to dial it down. They know how to recruit for the personality traits they don't have. And they also know how to build on the personality they do.

## Permissions of Mission

The greatest leaders are those liberated by purpose. They know why they are on the planet, and they are pursuing their life mission with determined enthusiasm. They have gained permission not just to lead; they also possess the freedom to live, really live. Knowing their mission and ordering their life and ministry around it grants these leaders certain key permissions.

### Meaning and Significance

"I'm having the time of my life," Karen responded when I asked how she was doing. Then Karen launched into a download of all the ways she was ministering from her new coffee-shop venue. Her stories included conversations with homeless people, business executives, and students. In these encounters God uses Karen to encourage people. Her entrée into their lives is her way of blessing them. When they ask the source of her obviously wonderful life view, she shares her own story of being radically transformed by Jesus. Karen prays each day and asks God to connect her with people who need his love and encouragement. "God just fills me up every time I help someone." Karen can't imagine doing anything else. For her, helping people never gets old. Her mission gives her permission to enjoy meaning and significance.

## Excellence

Leaders operating from a sense of mission care about not only what they do but how they do it. They pursue excellence, not for its own sake but for the sake of the mission that orders their lives. Pursuing excellence with this motive is not a burden; it is a privilege. It is not a pursuit of excellence born out of obsessive-compulsive perfectionist pathology. Great leaders feel profound gratitude to God for their opportunity to give their lives to the mission he has chosen for them. Practicing excellence for them is part of their grateful response to him. Their commitment to excellence shows up in as many ways as there are for leaders to pursue mission. It may be apparent in organizational processes of feeding people in community centers, training small-group leaders at church, or gaining maximum efficiencies in operational costs for a global missions enterprise.

"We want to model excellence—from how people are greeted, to the quality of our coffee, to the graphics displayed in our print material, to our Web site, to our worship experiences—everything we do." Garrett, a church planter, commented on his ministry while giving me a tour of his facilities. "We are committed to excellence because we want people to go, 'Wow!' when they come here. We want them to be intrigued in God." Excellence is not just a published core value of this congregation; it is indeed what people experience when they intersect this church ministry. The volunteers, not just church staff, evidence this commitment to excellence by the enthusiasm and competence they bring to their work. All this flows from a solid central mission that everyone shares now but that began in the heart and mind of that church planter.

Contrast this experience with the all-too-typical lack of commitment to excellence evidenced on the part of many organizations and ministry groups. Often you run into sloppy work, uninspired efforts, and a "whatever" attitude. When you do, you can be sure that they suffer from a lack of mission.

## Energy

Leaders on mission enjoy abundant energy, both in themselves and among those in their leadership team. The mission creates an energy supply that powers the leader through challenges and fills his or her sails when the trade winds are favorable.

"I got tired but I got over it!" Jeff quipped as we talked about his leadership in his missions organization. Jeff has responsibility for resourcing the dozens of church planters who are supported through his ministry. He exhibits an energy level that can't be explained merely in physical or physiological terms alone. Jeff is a dynamo because what he is doing is changing the world.

The kind of energy generated by missional focus is more than just the ability to go hard and long. It is also a quality of presence that allows the leader to "be there." It is a level of intensity that can only be sustained by a commitment to a great mission. Think of the apostle Paul's hoofing his way back into town after being stoned, or his singing at midnight after being beaten half to death, or preaching in chains to Agrippa. The apostle's great contribution to the Christian movement resulted, in part, from his indefatigable energy, the source of which was his mission to share the gospel.

Great leaders I have been around enjoy remarkable resiliency. Like all human beings they have their physical limits and grow bone weary at times. However, they bounce back quickly after rest, ready to get at it again. Their energies are not siphoned off by dealing with trivia (a leading cause of burnout in ministry), nor are they debilitated by distractions (a frequent problem in leaders and orga-nizations that are not mission-powered). The mission permits them to avoid the energy drains that beset many leaders.

## Intentionality

Jesus talked to his disciples about a choice between two roads. He said there is a broad way that leads to destruction and the narrow way that leads to life. We have tended to reduce Jesus' observation to a challenge involving people's choice of eternal destinies. Jesus probably had a much broader context in mind. He was talking about our decision to enter into abundant living—now! We can take the typical approach to life and leadership, doing just enough to respond to external stimuli and to conform to others' expecta-tions. If we do, we will get the quality of life chosen by the vast majority of people, including many leaders. This is a road to dimin-ished life, compared to the other path and its rewards.

The other destination—abundant life—is experienced when the leader chooses to live an intentional life. Intentionality in the leader results from a compelling sense of mission. Decisions about relationships, time, talent, money, direction, place of service, min-istry strategy—all these determinations are more intentional when powered and informed by a central life purpose.

I met with Ben and Frances to discuss the future of the ministry they had begun four years earlier. As they recounted their story, a pattern emerged: a pattern of disarray, of knee-jerk reactions or of veering right and left. Their target group had shifted; the location of their project had changed every few months, and their staff history was a revolving door of personnel moving in and out. The latest issue facing them was whether to make an entire shift in ministry methodology, moving away from an approach of inviting people to a worship service to a cell-based church. The obvious lack of intentionality in their work reflected the internal fuzziness of their personal mission. When I asked the simple question, "What do you want to do?" I got several minutes of rambling discourse.

There was no center. Consequently, they had no direction. Mission had eluded them; so had intentionality. The latest idea they encountered at a conference became the mission du jour.

Then there is David. He is serving a church in a community of under a thousand people in a town nobody has ever heard of. But when you go to lunch with him and hear him recount the work of God going on there, you would think his church is the epicenter of the Christian movement. He is starting prayer groups in restaurants, feeding the whole town at the local bar, remodeling the church, growing food to give away to the poor, and building a relationship with the African American pastors and churches in town (in the deep South).

David knows his mission: "to build a better town in the name of Jesus," as he puts it. He is intentional. And the abundant life he is experiencing will have you wondering whether you should pack up where you are and join him!

---

The power and permission of mission: significance, excellence, energy, and intentionality. All are gifts that great leaders enjoy.

# 5

# THE DISCIPLINE OF DECISION MAKING

Phil just couldn't make up his mind. The church he newly pastored had maxed out their facilities and needed to deal with the lack of space. The congregation had several options. They still had some room on their current property for expansion. Some in the congregation were pushing for consideration of multiple sites. Still others thought the pressure on the buildings could be lessened if they moved some church activities off-site, using small groups in homes for spiritual formation. A nice tract of land had also come on the market for a reasonable price in a growing part of the city, prompting some to favor a relocation strategy. Each option had its advantages—and its lobbying constituencies.

Phil knew that whatever decision the church made would write its future, in many ways defining the character of its mission in the next chapter of its ministry. Phil also knew that whatever course of action the church took would leave some people disappointed, not only in the decision but in the direction of the church. Some would probably leave because of their frustrations. Each scenario carried an element of risk. All parties were looking to Phil for leadership in reaching a decision.

As time went on, some key leaders began to grow impatient. They voiced concern that the momentum of the congregation would be lost unless they chose a direction. But Phil couldn't make a determination in his own mind. His overcautiousness paralyzed him. He just couldn't decide. Phil also missed the opportunity to be a great leader.

Randy was just the opposite. It didn't take him long to make a decision at all. At first his followers liked that because they thought it signaled confidence. But Randy *always* made quick decisions, whether or not a quick decision was needed or prudent. His impatience at studying options led him to make impulsive decisions that proved costly, both for his followers and for him. His diminishing leadership line of credit eventually would not cover the checks he was writing with the decisions he was making. A meeting of the governing board was called, with Randy's leadership style as the sole agenda item. Once he felt the heat was on, Randy characteristically made a quick decision. He abruptly resigned rather than undergo reflection on the decision-making practices that had undermined his leadership competence.

Careth provided good leadership to her ministry team in so many ways. She recruited well, made assignments appropriate to people's talent and experiences, and articulated a compelling vision that energized her efforts and the energies of those around her. But she frustrated her followers with her tendency to make a decision, only to change her mind. Often one staff member would leave from a meeting with Careth, feeling clear about a course of action that had been decided upon, only to receive different instructions later. Some staff members remarked that they wanted to be the last person to talk to Careth about an issue, since the last person's input seemed to be the deciding factor in determining her response. Her team responded by becoming tentative in their commitment and action. Careth and her team lost the chance to be a great team.

Brett simply couldn't stay focused. Everybody knew it, so they sought ways to work around it every way they could. The elders hired an administrator. They established accountabilities for Brett's assignments in an effort to coach him on finishing projects he started. His outstanding communication skills and brilliant mind enabled him to be effective in identifying possibilities and persuading people to join the cause. Unfortunately, these people didn't realize they were joining the cause du jour. Brett himself came to grips with his inability to stay the course, realizing that his shortcoming exhausted the energies of followers and threatened to keep the ministry organization in perpetual chaos. He eventually chose a leadership role that took him out of the driver position.

These leaders all represent a vast number of leaders who have trouble making decisions. Either they have difficulty making the right decision, or they second-guess themselves once they've made a decision. In many cases they simply can't focus on the particular decision that should command their attention.

Great leaders know how to make decisions, when to make decisions, and what decisions need to be made. They exercise consistently good judgment. While they don't always make the right decisions, they do so often enough that they enjoy significant accomplishments in their leadership agendas and gain important credibility with their followers.

## Elements of Good Decision Making

Great leaders consider six key elements when making decisions. They may not proceed through these elements in a linear analysis; usually, they are working on several fronts at once. And leaders may not be aware of dealing with each concern, particularly if their decision-making style is highly intuitive. However, great leaders did not arrive at their level of competence without paying attention to these requirements for making good decisions.

### Ask the Right Questions

Good decision makers make sure they are working on answering the right question. They know that answering the wrong question, even precisely, doesn't accomplish anything; in fact, it keeps leaders and organizations tied up in counterproductive pursuits, with potentially disastrous results.

> Pastor Ned finally realized that changing the worship style and moving the worship times at his church were the wrong problems for him to be working on. This realization came only after he had paid a terrible price personally in terms of the conflict generated by his new initiatives. He had endured months of criticism from church members who resisted the changes before they happened, as he nurtured the hope that the new worship would draw many new faces into the church, making all the pain worthwhile. Trouble is, it didn't happen. Now, four months into the new schedule and services, he was looking at the same faces—actually, fewer of those faces.
>
> Ned finally came to grips with the real issue: the congregation's lack of mission. The right question involved helping the church gain God's heart for people, especially those who have yet to hear the gospel of God's redemptive love. Absent this conviction, the church members just viewed the worship and schedule changes as a loss for them.

This beleaguered pastor is not alone. All over North America churches and church leaders are busy addressing the wrong questions. Answering them not only won't address the critical issues facing them, it will, in fact, compound the wider church's dilemma and hasten its slide into spiritual obsolescence in the emerging culture. Given the significant collapse of the influence of the church in American culture, and given the fact that church attendance is holding up only because people are living longer, and given the signs of heightened spiritual awareness accompanied by a loss of affection for religious institutions, and given how God is working in other parts of the world where Pentecost is happening every hour, you might think that North American church leaders would be scrambling to deal with the real issues underlying these realities. Instead, many continue to deal only with presenting problems, fed by short-sighted hopes of making their church successful, and are thus working themselves into mental, physical, emotional, and spiritual exhaustion in pursuit of answers to the wrong questions.

A list of these wrong questions, juxtaposed with the tough questions that church leaders *should* be addressing, points out how very different the leader's agenda will be shaped, depending on the question he is addressing.[6]

> *Wrong question:* How do we "do church" better?
> *Tough question:* How do we "be church" better? Or how do we deconvert from "churchianity" (institutional religion) to Christianity (the movement)?

> *Wrong question:* How do we grow this church?
> *Tough question:* How do we serve this community?

> *Wrong question:* How do we develop ministers for the church?
> *Tough question:* How do we develop missionaries to the culture?

> *Wrong question:* How do we develop church members?
> *Tough question:* How do we develop followers of Jesus?

> *Wrong question:* How do we plan for the future we see?
> *Tough question:* How do we prepare for the future God sees?

> *Wrong question:* How do we develop leaders for church work?
> *Tough question:* How do we develop leaders for the Christian movement?

The ability to ask the right question requires that spiritual leaders spend more time thinking beyond the presenting problems, peering under the hood, so to speak, to see the real issues. They must be willing to challenge the status quo and to be ruthless in their analysis of both the situation and the results. Great spiritual leaders are aided in this search by their constant discipline of learning. This is one area where breadth of knowledge becomes indispensable. For instance, a pastor savvy in transition issues understands why people are resistant to change, so he knows to provide emotional support to people, not just arguments to convince them of the necessity for change. A smart leader begins with people's sense of loss, not their recalcitrance.

The requirement that spiritual leaders grasp the right question also pushes them toward God. The prayer life of great spiritual leaders is oftentimes centered on asking God to help them understand what is happening around them. Contrast this to a typical approach to prayer that informs God about what is going on and then asks for his help or intervention. Great spiritual leaders have God's view of a situation. This enables them to partner with him in bringing about the future God desires. This powerful prayer life is not accidental. It requires a commitment and discipline on the part of the leader to listen in prayer, not just talk.

## Get Enough of the Right Kind of Information

Many leaders make poor decisions, either because they did not have adequate information or because they chose to ignore the information at their disposal. The causes for this range from a lack of intelligence about what's going on in the organization to mishandling the information the leader has at his or her disposal. Simply said, the leader's access to adequate information depends on paying attention to both external and internal voices.

Barry pushed ahead, despite the consultant's report. Determined to turn around the ministry from its five-year revenue decline, he proposed to his board that they launch a new venture that would be designed to create a new customer base. At the board's suggestion Barry contracted with a consulting firm to conduct a feasibility study. Two problems with the proposal surfaced. The first related to the cost of the project. The new ministry venture would require a massive technology infusion and upgrade. Second, the existing customer base reacted with lukewarm enthusiasm to the new resource. For the project to succeed, a new customer base would have to be cultivated at the risk of alienating existing customers, since resources would be reallocated from existing customer service to support the new ministry platform. The consultant's recommendation was to put the project on hold.

Determined to go forward with the project anyway, Barry made an impassioned plea to the board, arguing that the risk was manageable and implying, not too subtly, that their faith needed to rise to the level of his personal vision from God. The board reluctantly went along. It was the wrong decision. Costs of the technology were underestimated. Existing customers turned to other providers who gave them what they wanted. New customers never materialized. The venture flopped. By the time Barry was finally asked to resign, the financial straits of the ministry made the project no longer viable.

Having adequate information can make the difference in whether a leader survives or not.

Pastor Jerry smelled a rat. The demands presented to him by a rogue group of self-appointed leaders did not appear, on the surface, to be an adequate reason for the drastic action they were calling for. Jerry had been caught flat-footed by the group who appeared in his office one afternoon to share some concerns, as well as a petition for him to step down as pastor. In a hastily convened meeting of senior congregational leaders, Jerry found out that no one had any "intelligence" on the situation. This signaled to him that the operation was covert. Upon further investigation the pastor discovered that a staff member had been acting as a saboteur for months, undermining his leadership in a campaign to oust Jerry in a hostile takeover. Had the pastor accepted things at face value and not pushed for more information, he would have become an unwilling coconspirator in his own demise.

Leaders who want adequate information have to make sure they are connected to the ministry organization at all levels. Interestingly, this often becomes harder to maintain, the longer the leader's tenure. Far too typically, leaders tend to gather a group of cronies; in about five years, most leaders have insulated themselves from new sources of information. They return to their trusted advisers again and again, even though these advisers may no longer be the best sources for information or perspective on the ministry organization. The leader is the victim of being underinformed or the recipient of skewed information. That's why it is so vital that leaders continue to solicit new voices.

Staying connected requires that a leader work the phones, intentionally seeking information, actually listening to what others are saying. Too many leaders forego good information because their mouths are too open and in motion. They are in a selling mode when they should be in a listening (buying) mode. Exceptional leaders actually pay attention to the information they receive, especially if it indicates the situation is not as they imagine it. How the leader handles cognitive dissonance determines whether or not aides and coworkers will offer insights that challenge a view or course of action. Not paying attention to information can be deadly. Just ask George Custer. His scouts told him he was in poor position to pick a fight. Custer's arrogance in the face of good information cost him more than his leadership position. Unfortunately, others also paid supremely for his mishandling of the information available to him.

Wise leaders also understand their personal cognitive processes and the role they play in their decision-making style. Some leaders are external in their cognitive style, meaning they go "outside" themselves in order to gain information and to make decisions. They do this through debate and discussion, through listening sessions, through think tanks, by hashing things out verbally. This style can get them adequate information if they choose their sources well and stay open to others' input.

Many leaders, on the other hand, are internal processors who go "into" themselves to figure out what they think. They read, write position papers, and commission others to write reports for their review and consideration; they study, pray, and noodle on things in isolation. The challenge for these leaders is to force themselves to gain adequate information for their decision making. The followers of internal leaders can often feel frustrated in their ability to provide information; they may not even be aware of what their leaders are working on inside their head. By the time a decision is announced, it is often too late to influence the leaders' thinking.

Are you listening? Who are you listening to? Where is their information coming from? Are you open for conflicting advice? Are you connected? These questions are critical issues for leaders who want to secure adequate information for the present and into the future.

When Jesus asked his disciples, "Who do people say that I am?" he was not just trying to get some more scripture written. When he followed up his disciples' responses with, "Who do you say that I am?" he had not adopted an argumentative, persuasive posture. He was honestly gauging how his message was coming across, both with the public and with his most trusted followers. This information helped him know how to calibrate his message and his methods to achieve his mission. If Jesus went to such lengths to gain good information, mere human spiritual leaders surely have to do the same.

## Consider Timing

Timing is very significant in spiritual leadership. The Bible speaks often of the importance of time. Paul indicated that timing played a role in the timetable for the Incarnation ("But when the time had fully come, God sent his son" [Galatians 4:4, NIV]). Timing played a major role in shaping Jesus' ministry and death. Not only would Jesus not go to the cross for the wrong reasons. He didn't go until it was the right time ("Jesus knew that the time had come for him to leave this world and go to the Father" [John 13:1, NIV]).

Great leaders understand the importance of timing, specifically when it comes to making decisions. There are right times to consider issues and right times to make moves. Conversely, even the right issue tackled at the wrong time faces certain defeat.

There is no formula for great timing. It is part instinct, part intuition, part paying attention to surroundings, part prayer life, and all of the above. It is not guesswork. Leaders who have a good sense of timing seem very wired into their situations while, at the same time, wired into God for a perspective that transcends just what the leader and his or her advisers can see. Leaders adept at timing know how to read audiences and situations. They have practiced this over the years, testing out their hunches and intuitions. They have learned how to monitor their own internal sensors and when to pay attention to the voices around them and the voice within. Leaders with great timing know how to test the water, sniff the wind, and commit just enough to gauge reaction before committing it all. They risk, but they do not gamble.

> The pastor of a large urban church defied conventional wisdom: he consolidated the number of worship services to just one when the congregation moved into freshly renovated space. After a year of being dislocated from their worship center, he felt the church's sense of community would be well served by being together. The spirit of the services went sky high. The atmosphere for the next months was electric. Four months later he announced a move back to multiple services. He wanted to do it before people's new routines became set. Both calls were made by a savvy leader who is a pro at understanding timing in leadership.

Sometimes the leader is ready to make a decision, but other people need time to catch up.

> Leigh knew that her ministry role was coming to an end in the organization she had joined six years earlier. She was not distressed with her current assignment; she simply felt called to another city to become a part of some ministry there. Yet she

knew that timing was going to be important. For two years she prayed about when to leave. Every time she felt the urge to announce her departure, she resisted it. She discerned that though she was ready to move on, some facets of her world were not yet completed, either in the organization she was leaving or in something God was preparing for her. Leigh's decision to hold off was confirmed when an unforeseen crisis emerged that she was uniquely qualified to handle. After the crisis, Leigh sensed that the timing was now right for her to resign and move. When she did, she almost immediately discovered a group of people who had only recently begun to pray for God to send someone with Leigh's technical skills to launch their new ministry. The timing was perfect—God's and Leigh's.

## Involve the Right People

Sometimes the right intentions of leaders fail because the right people do not get involved in the decision-making process.

Governor David Beasley scheduled a prime-time telecast to the people of South Carolina. He announced that he had formed the conviction that the Confederate flag needed to come off the flagpole atop the statehouse dome. The governor demonstrated great moral, spiritual, and political courage with his declaration. The only problem was that the decision about the whereabouts of the Confederate flag did not rest with him. The issue would be decided in the General Assembly—the legislative body of the state. In his rush to share his heart-felt spiritual burden, the young governor failed to build a coalition of supporters who could rally to his cause and push the issue through the General Assembly. The result was costly. Under pressure, the General Assembly adopted a miserable compromise, removing the flag from the dome, only to place it on a prominent place on the statehouse grounds. Governor Beasley also suffered politically. Many analysts attribute his lost reelection bid to his stance on the flag issue.

Getting the right people involved proves critical for good decision making. Effective leaders think through the following categories of people when working through decisions:

**Key Leaders.**  The leadership corps of the organization provides the leader with insight on the front end of decisions and support after the decision is made.

**Legitimizers.**  Every organization, particularly congregational systems, contains certain influential people who "legitimize" the leader, usually through their public expressions of approval. Legitimizers gain their status in a variety of ways. Sometimes it is through family connections, longevity of involvement, political clout, community status, financial position, or previous leadership roles they have played. They do not necessarily need to be part of the leadership corps.

Legitimizer support proves crucial during those times when the leader is embarking on new ventures or changing directions, especially if there is risk of significant resistance. It is also important in periods of significant tension or bewilderment over a leader's decision (often regarding personnel matters that cannot be discussed publicly) or times when the leader is under attack.

Betsy had been forced to let a popular staff leader go due to immorality. She was not at liberty to discuss her rationale with the congregation when she announced the staff leader's departure. People were shocked, some obviously distressed. In the wake of the announcement Betsy called on Flynn, the congregational patriarch, to pray. Flynn turned the occasion into a show of support for Betsy by saying she had made the tough, but right, decision. In his prayer he asked for understanding on the part of those who had incomplete information. In five minutes Flynn defused the situation by legitimizing Betsy's decision.

**Veto Holders.**  Veto holders are those people in an organizational system who can kill an idea just by signaling their disapproval of it.

They often gain their position of influence the same way legitimizers do, but they use their power to block decisions. In some cases they maintain their role through intimidation. Effective leaders often work to develop relationships with these influencers for the sake of gaining additional leadership leverage. Veto holders do not have to be consulted on every decision, but if the decision is significant, ignoring them risks wasting major leadership capital. At times it is not possible to gain their assent, but the leader can get them to agree not to obstruct the decision.

I well remember one experience with veto holders. I arrived late in the afternoon to meet with the pastor prior to the congregational meeting that was to be held that evening. He briefed me on the months of conflict that had precipitated the current crisis in his leadership. I then met with other leaders of the congregation. I found that the two sides were not as far apart as both had initially indicated. I secured from congregational leaders a pledge to work toward some key compromise positions I felt the pastor would accept.

When I went back to him to debrief the congregational meeting, he agreed to the proposal. Then he said, "It won't matter what we agree to unless the judge okays it."

"Which one was he?" I asked.

"Oh, he wasn't here. He's not a member of the church, but what he says goes in this town."

"What has he said to you about this situation?" I probed.

The pastor snorted, "I'm not about to talk to him about church business. He's not a member."

"I suggest you have coffee with him," I said.

The pastor didn't. The compromise fell through. The pastor was forced to leave. With the judge's approval. It pays to pay attention to those with veto power, regardless of where they are in the congregational system.

**Implementers.**  A decision without implementation is a waste of leadership resources. It makes great sense to involve in decision making those people who will be doing the work and making things happen. They not only know what's doable and reasonable, they are usually much closer to solutions than people whose involvement is limited to conceptual chatter and ideological debate.

> The properties committee of the congregation promulgated a new facilities-use policy for outside groups. Their new procedures caused enormous dilemmas for the staff, from audio technicians to office personnel, to the janitorial crew. None of these people had been consulted in the decision. In the aftermath of the debacle, the committee asked for staff suggestions. The result was a much more workable approach that could be implemented by the people who were actually doing all the heavy lifting.

*Those Affected by the Decision.*   Great decision makers seek out the involvement of the people who will live with the decision. Their perspective may be entirely different from those charged with making decisions. While this dynamic seems so obvious, it is often ignored by those whose decisions turn out to be less than stellar. For example, committees of my denomination's executive board wrestled for months with a financial crisis with one of our institutions for the elderly. Discussion ranged from philosophical issues of whether we should be involved in operating retirement centers to practical issues of economics and management. Trustees then sought input from residents of our two retirement homes—arguably the people most affected by whatever decision was to be made. We were all amazed to see the way the residents galvanized statewide support through their relational networks, including raising hundreds of thousands of dollars. Their inclusion in the decision-making process changed the entire debate, at least in the short term. The discussion went from trying to figure out how to shut these homes down to trying to figure out how to keep them open.

## Operate with the Right Motives

Those who follow great leaders trust the leaders' motives. These leaders gain this trust, in part, because their decisions reflect those motives. Others can clearly see how the leaders' decisions seek their well-being. Decisions that seem politically expeditious or designed to benefit the leaders' self-interest diminish the trust level. Decisions that appear petty or selfish or punitive reveal motives that eventually undermine leaders' capacity to lead effectively. Impure motives do more than cloud leaders' judgment in decision making. They set back the kingdom of God.

Harry had a bad case of the "wannabes." He made sure to be at the right place at the right time with the right people. He worked the phones to be politically connected in his denomination, to be a player in its leadership circles. Harry's sermons became full of personal stories in which Harry usually played the role of hero or the wise mentor to others who turned to him for advice. He fudged the numbers on denominational reporting, covering up a decline in church attendance. At the same time, he led the church to purchase a huge tract of land for expansion and to assume a debt way beyond prudent levels. Congregational leaders who began to question his decisions were banished. An initial trickle of disaffection eventually became a steady stream of people leaving the church. The consistent refrain of these saddened people was they could no longer trust the pastor.

Pastor Evan exhibited a different set of motives in his decision making. For several years he worked tirelessly to find a relocation option for the growing congregation, but when they finally found a site, they realized that they would have to scale back their building plans due to the increased cost of the land. The redrawn facilities design didn't capture the imagination of the members or generate the enthusiasm earlier dreams had excited. Evan polled the congregation and found a willingness to move ahead, despite their disappointment. Evan nevertheless felt he did not have the overwhelming vote of confidence that was necessary for the project to succeed, so he called off the move. There was a corporate sigh of relief. Congregational members knew that Evan had set aside his own ambitions in order to preserve the integrity of the church's decision-making processes that had always valued unity. Consequently, Evan's leadership grew in the eyes of his followers. They knew his motives were right.

Evan went to work raising additional funds and continuing to develop more appealing building plan options. A year later, when Evan again brought the issue to the congregation, they voted unanimously to relocate. They had the confidence in Evan's decision because they trusted him to do the right thing. This trust was informed by their experience of Evan's leadership.

## Understand Intended Outcomes

Many leaders come up short in realizing their dreams because they never move past the dream phase. They fail to do the hard work of asking, How would we know if we made the right decision? Excellent decision makers know what they are trying to accomplish with their deliberations. Their clear understanding of the results they are after clarifies their thinking. They have determined their scorecard. Without this awareness of outcomes, leaders have no way of knowing when they are winning. Even worse, without a clear scorecard leaders might not even know what game they are playing. For instance, a church-growth scorecard and a missional-church scorecard are very different. In fact, the church-growth scorecard can beat up a leader who is trying to lead his followers to be missional.

Charlotte skillfully guided her ministry team to redesign their scorecard, based on the new vision God had given them. The results she anticipated were clearly spelled out. For instance, staff was going to be held accountable for developing relationships with community leaders in order to partner more with them in ministering to the city. Every unit in the church (Sunday School class, small group, music ensemble, and so on) was chartered to design a community outreach project. The percentage of money in the budget going into local ministries was dramatically increased. Every staff member thought through their ministry activities and programs and detailed exactly how they were going to integrate into them the new missional initiatives.

Because Charlotte did the hard work of detailing the end game, the decisions she and others had to make crystallized more easily. Staff time had to be redirected, resources had to be redistributed, some previous activities had to be curtailed or cancelled, and ministry constituents had to be challenged to rethink their personal contributions to the work. Although many of the decisions were difficult, they made sense, given the intended results, and so Charlotte's organization could embrace them.

Elements of good decision making include addressing the right question, obtaining adequate information, sensing the appropriateness of the timing, getting the right people involved, operating from proper motives, and knowing the intended results. Practicing better decision making requires effective leaders to acquire these elements in preparing for their deliberations.

## Debriefing Decisions

Great decision making doesn't stop with having the right elements. It also requires getting adequate feedback during the process to monitor the impact of the decision. And the very best leaders learn from their own decision-making performance. They debrief their decisions, that is, they question and examine their thinking and the other ingredients in a decision. They don't do this occasionally or episodically. They routinely debrief decisions and ministry experience as a strategy and as part of their practice of leadership.

Jesus employed this strategy in the development and deployment of his band of disciples. After sending them out on mission (Luke 9 and 10), he pulled them aside to debrief their experiences, both for their development and for him to gain feedback on his work. The disciples reported on the response of people and demons.

They answered Jesus' questions about public perceptions of him and his mission. Jesus helped them assign meaning to all they were seeing and experiencing.

Debriefing decisions involves asking a series of questions. This investigation can be pursued by the leader in a group or team setting, especially if the team was involved in the decision or its implementation or if the leader wants to elicit feedback beyond his or her own perceptions. The questions will parallel the same concerns we have already identified in discussing the elements of good decision making:

*"Why did I have to make this decision?"* This question explores the reasons a decision was called for. It may have been the result of previous decisions or even previous indecisions. This inquiry also forces you to examine your own role in the decision-making process. Should you have implicated yourself into the decision at all? Could others have made it? Why did the decision reach the level of requiring your attention?

Many leaders make too many decisions. If they asked themselves why they needed to make a decision more often, they might realize that they should offload some decision-making responsibilities to others. Their overinvolvement in decision making might result from poor delegation skills, inadequate staffing, incompetent staff, or a need for control on their part.

*"Did I answer the wrong question?"* Getting an answer to this probe may take some time to sort out. Whenever you get poor results, or unexpected results, or experience unanticipated repercussions from your decisions, you might suspect this to be the issue. Great leaders are always evaluating the issues they are working on; they want to make sure they are focused on the right questions.

*"Was the timing right?"* In debriefing decisions you will want to search for clues you may have noticed and remember why you missed them, in hopes of being more attuned to timing issues in the future. Were you too far ahead of your followers? Lagging too far

behind? Did you miss the window of opportunity or catch the wave? Why or why not?

*"Did I get the right people involved?"* The answer to this question will be obvious, based on people's responses. Do you have their support or not? Do you have enough hands on deck to turn the decision into reality, or is there an obvious lack of buy-in? Who could have helped you? Who did help you? You don't want to forget people in either category.

*"Did I act or react?"* This is your self-assessment of your psychological responses in your decision making. Were your hot buttons getting punched? Was someone jerking your chain? Did you surrender your considered and deliberate analysis to knee-jerk reactions? Were you getting even, getting ahead, getting too emotionally involved? Or did you act in the best interest of your ministry organization?

*"Did I generate enough options?"* Great decision makers resist the temptation to lock in on a course of action too soon. They create and consider multiple options, even ones they don't personally favor, to make sure enough creative juice has gone into seeking solutions. Keeping multiple options on the table also encourages debate and dialogue. The way people on your leadership team respond varies greatly, depending on their perception of whether you are genuinely seeking input for a decision or merely advocating a decision you have already made.

*"What outcomes did I achieve?"* You always want to evaluate the results of your decisions. Calibrate these against what you anticipated. This will help your leadership vision in the future. Did you determine how you would gauge your success, the impact of your decision? Asking and answering this question will also help you know what decisions require follow-up action.

NASA debriefs its missions. Military officers debrief their operations. Spiritual leaders must be no less committed to learning from their decisions. Debriefing as a practice will not make your decision-making capability perfect, but it will significantly enhance your decision-making acumen.

## Learning from Mistakes

Let's face it. You will blow some decisions. That goes with the territory of being a leader. You will need to challenge some very pervasive ideas and adopt some key stances to enable your leadership to grow through mistakes.

### Move Past Success-Failure Thinking

The truth is, life is not neat or compartmentalized. Successes can come with downsides. Failures may, and often do, carry in them the seeds of success. It is better to view leadership triumphs and tragedies along a continuum. While certain events fall closer to one pole than the other, the leadership saga goes on. It is better to talk in terms of direction rather than static categories. You are not a success or a failure. The jury is still out. The verdict is not yet in. The outcome depends on you.

> Travis's first attempt at launching an online leadership-development delivery system failed, due to some unanticipated glitches in the technology. The result was an overpromised, underdelivered service. Six months later Travis "rebooted" the system with a new program that was more modest in its promises but doable. Innovative technologies, Travis understood, are always disruptive. This realization helped him put the episode in perspective. Rather than feel defeated with his first failed attempt, Travis decided to view it as a learning experience.

### Practice Self-Differentiation

Erik slumped in his seat as he ended the phone call. The church member on the other end had just unloaded on him about the shortcomings of the student ministry. Erik's despondency was fed by a strong sense that he had personally failed to provide a good student ministry. The truth was, dozens of people, including several professional staff members, had frontline responsibility for student ministry. Yet Erik went beyond feeling responsible. He interpreted this criticism as an indictment of him and his ministry. He felt like a failure.

One of the key psychological and developmental stages for spiritual leaders is to separate their personal identity from their ministry—a state that is known as self-differentiation. Many leaders seem unable to achieve this. They so identify with their ministry organization that they see it as an extension of themselves. While it is true that our ministries reflect our personalities, our priorities, our personal passions, it is not healthy to see ourselves completely tied up in the organization's performance. It is not healthy for leaders to view every failure in an organization as personal failure.

Truthfully, leaders who fail to develop and to practice self-differentiation from their ministries often derail in their leadership. They tend not to develop other leaders because they cannot trust others to perform their tasks well. This is self-defeating, because the effect of this decision is to shrink the ministry down to the level where the leader can take care of everything. Failure-tolerant leaders know that other people have to take responsibility and will make mistakes. Not every mistake is a reflection on their leadership.

## Give Up on Perfectionism

Perfectionism plagues and paralyzes some spiritual leaders.

Ramon beat himself up with every wrong decision. Every one. He somehow felt he should have done a better job anticipating circumstances, other people's reactions, and the impact of the options he chose. Despite the oft-received advice from coworkers and friends, Ramon never cut himself any slack. Any wrong call on his part precipitated a round of self-flagellation.

Perfectionism is the enemy of grace. Even those of us who preach grace sometimes fail to afford it to ourselves. It doesn't help to say that you don't expect of others any more than you expect of yourself if you are expecting too much from yourself. There is an insidious idolatry at the heart of perfectionism: a belief that we can be without fault, a belief that we can *be* God. This should not be construed as an argument for sloppiness or laziness. However, we simply have to come to grips with the fact that we are human, and human beings sometimes lack judgment and make the wrong call. Some spiritual leaders say this, but deep down they put themselves on a pedestal. It hurts to fall from up there. And you will fall.

———————

Merely believing you are on a great mission does not guarantee success. Making good decisions does. Great leaders understand this. They know how crucial good decision making is. That's why they practice making better decisions relentlessly. It becomes a leadership and life discipline for them. While others are dreaming and jawing, they are making decisions that change the world.

# 6

# THE DISCIPLINE
# OF BELONGING

Leadership is lonely. But it can be less lonely than many spiritual leaders make it.

Great leaders in the Bible were hardly loners. Moses, perhaps the most solitary of them, still maintained significant connections, particularly with family. We are not told how he stayed in touch with his family of origin during the days of being raised an Egyptian prince or the forty years of tending sheep with the Midianite desert clan. But brother Aaron and sister Miriam played an important role in Moses' leadership team. Moses also apparently enjoyed a particularly close relationship with Jethro, his father-in-law, who really served as Moses' father figure. Not only did Jethro provide Moses with a job and a wife when he was a fugitive from Pharaoh's Egypt, he also gave Moses good management advice that kept the Exodus from derailing. As Moses' leadership extended into the wilderness years, he formed close connections with Joshua, who would succeed him as leader.

David's bond with Jonathan was legendary, but it was not the only significant relationship of his life. Though his family of origin seemed to provide little support for his ascendance as a leader (they must not have been paying attention when Samuel visited Jesse's house to anoint the young shepherd-singer), others rallied to him throughout his life. His band of faithful men protected him and prosecuted his military agenda. Nathan the prophet got close enough to challenge the king's actions (something not very easy to do in a near-Eastern despot's court). Obviously, David inspired incredible loyalty and devotion among those in his circle.

Paul developed an extensive network of friends and coworkers in the churches he founded across Asia Minor and into Europe. His letters are replete with personal references, revealing more than a casual acquaintance with those he named. The apostle also managed a personal entourage that traveled with him on his missionary journey. Barnabas, John Mark, Luke, Timothy, Silas, are just some of his traveling companions. They served in a variety of capacities, from sponsor (Barnabas) to partner (Silas) to chronicler-physician (Luke) to mentoree (Timothy). Paul's insistence on Christians connecting with each other and tending to those connections formed some of the major pastoral themes of his correspondence. This concern grew out of the way he conducted his own life and ministry.

Jesus not only connected with the masses; he enjoyed abiding relationships with special people in his life. The profound connection with his mother, Mary, has inspired religious devotion to her among his followers, as well as provided artists, composers, and sculptors with inspiration for some of the best-known works of art in the world. Jesus also cultivated a relationship with his cousin John the Baptist, launching his public ministry with a visit to him and communicating with him when John was imprisoned. The Bethany trio of Mary, Martha, and Lazarus also formed a tender bond with Jesus. It is no accident that Jesus spent his last weekend on earth with these friends. Their nurture steeled him for Passion Week.

Then there were those disciples. With the whole world to save, Jesus decided to create a community of close followers to whom he would entrust the movement. Jesus' teaching about belonging, being connected to God, and loving people are all modeled in his remarkably connected life.[7]

## Drawing Lessons from a Quantum Universe

Quantum physics provides the underlying scientific foundation for the postmodern world, just as Newtonian physics supplied the understanding of the universe that supported the modern era.

Quantum scientists have a different view of the created order from that of their predecessors. In the modern world the universe was treated like a giant thing—a gargantuan machine, really—that could be torn apart for observation and analysis. The assumption was that if we could understand the parts we could understand the whole. And if we could explain how it worked, we didn't need God. Modernity attacked the supernatural, determined to drain mystery out of the universe, eventually replacing it with skepticism. The modern world's epochal achievement was the splitting of the atom—the ultimate rendering asunder of the basic "building block" of the universe.

Scientists of the quantum variety see the universe not as a giant thing but as a complex network of relationships. Take, for instance, quantum physicists' discoveries of the atomic structure. They have now discovered a host of subatomic particles that populate the subatomic universe (quarks, muons, gluons, weak gauge bosons, gravitons, and photons make up a much more detailed set of elements than the three I grew up with: protons, neutrons, and electrons). Nuclear physicists now say that inner space is as infinite as outer space, with more subatomic particles being discovered all the time. None of these particles exist in isolation. They are all in relationship with other particles. This is the fundamental reason quantum physics sees everything as connected.

This notion of connectivity finds expression in the World Wide Web. Both "worldwide" and "web" underscore the proximity we share, no matter how spatially separated we might be. Two or three clicks and we are "there." In quantum spirituality, postmoderns assume they are connected to God and to other people. This poses an intriguing dilemma to spiritual tribes whose evangelism strategy begins with the declaration to people that they are separated from God!

Community is also one of the themes of the emerging missional church. As opposed to a worldview and ministry approach where the church could exist practically unconnected to its surrounding community (and many do!), the missional church is turned outward toward its community. Missional congregations and their leaders strategize ways to connect with people who are not a part of their congregation. Again, a sense of collective "belonging" permeates this approach.

A kingdom theology is also in ascendancy that helps missional congregations see themselves as part of the larger work of God in the world. This stands in sharp contrast to the perspective of many in the old church culture who practiced church as a "silo" religious experience isolated (and insulated) from the rest of the world, with the church considered to be both the focus and recipient. A kingdom view sees God's redemptive mission being carried out in the world (extended beyond the church culture).

Spiritual leaders who want to practice greatness today operate within the quantum universe, emphasizing connectivity, belonging, and community. The insight that the universe exists as a series of relationships is not news to them. After all, the central tenet of Christian theology is that God exists in community. Father, Son, and Spirit enjoy a relationship that has spilled out into the created order, all the way into the subatomic region. The search for belonging is part of what it means for humans to be created in the image of God. People need each other. We are relational beings. We not only want to belong, we only come to a true understanding of who we are in our relationships with God and with other people. We must belong to be fully alive.

Leaders who aspire to greatness not only preach these truths to those who follow them; they practice belonging in their own life. Common expressions of this community in their lives include family, friends, coworkers, mentors, and followers. Leaders obviously do not experience the same level of community in each of these types of connections. Their relationships are not spread out equally across these groups. In fact, they may have one or more areas that do not reflect substantial connectivity for them. This is fairly typical. However, these leaders are profoundly connected at some level. That connectivity, that belonging, grounds them in a way that grants them security in who they are and nurtures them for the journey they are on.

## Belonging to Family

"I've just hit a wall," pastor Stewart said to me over the phone. "I have been at my church for six years. We've done great, still are. New people are coming, folks are excited. But I'm just out of gas. I think I'm burned out."

"What is your wife saying to you about this?" I probed.

"Not anything, really," he replied.

"What is she saying to you about you, then?" I pressed.

A long pause followed, then in a measured way he said, "We've got a communication problem. We really don't talk much. We haven't for years." Now that the gates were open, he poured out years of marriage frustration, including lack of physical affection, loss of emotional connection, even a suspected affair.

"Stewart," I said, "you and I can talk about ministry burnout and probably should, eventually. But treating you without treating your marriage would ignore the larger problem. If there's a slow leak in your marriage, your emotional life is depleted. Your ministry burnout may be a symptom of this, or you may be throwing your energy into ministry as an escape to keep from dealing with your marriage issues. Either way, we need to focus on your home first." Stewart agreed to see a therapist to begin working on addressing his relationship with his life partner.

For spiritual leaders what's happening at home plays a huge role in supporting their leadership. While this dynamic is true for leaders in all sectors, it is especially true in the spiritual arena. The reason for this is the expectation that spiritual leadership should exhibit high integrity. This integrity begins with the correspondence between what leaders espouse and what they actually practice in their own lives. Simply said, the walk should match the talk. That starts at home where we are most exposed, where we are known for who we are. Somehow, if genuine spirituality doesn't show up here, any claims to spirituality can hardly be considered genuine.

I do not intend to imply that leaders should have perfect marriages, perfect kids, and perfect homes. One of the unfortunate characteristics of the North American Church culture is its perfectionist tendencies and the resulting loss of genuine community. It is hard to be real when you are punished for vulnerability or when the only reward comes for perceived flawlessness. Too many spiritual leaders have been treated inappropriately or even driven out of the ministry for having wayward kids or nonsupportive spouses, as if the leader is responsible for and makes all the decisions for every family member, including teenagers and young adults who choose behaviors that do not align with biblical values. The Bible and human history are full of stories of great spiritual leaders who had pretty rough home lives (does David come to mind?). If perfection were the requirement for spiritual leadership, the ranks would be thinned out—completely!

The point of this discussion is that for many great leaders, their home provides a place of genuine belonging and community. And if we all had our way, we would want to experience home as that safe place where we are known and loved the best. I have yet to meet a leader who wishes otherwise. Unfortunately, it is not always possible, and the leader has to satisfy his search for belonging in other ways.

Taking the suggestions that follow can maximize your capacity for belonging in your family:

• *As much as possible, you want to be at peace with your family of origin.* Sometimes issues of abuse or physical separation severely limit this option. The point is not to let unfinished business create problems for your ability to establish and to enjoy intimacy and belonging in other relationships. Push for healing if it is necessary, even if it has to be all one-sided. Many of us, even when not confronting major challenges, would wish something were different about our family of origin, but since we can't change them, identify and celebrate the good gifts. Don't obsess over the shortcomings. Don't impose on your family of origin inappropriate expectations that you would not want placed on you by your own children as they eventually evaluate your influence on them.

• *If you are married, determine to work for intimacy with your spouse.* This includes not just physical intimacy but that weaving together of lives so tightly that "when one cries, the other tastes salt." God's gift of marriage intended this experience for human couples. The chance to journey through life with a soul mate is worth whatever effort is required. No one who has it would swap it for the world. This level of human intimacy does not come absent risk or pain. It does not develop because there have been no bumps or disappointments or failed expectations; it comes despite them. Soul intimacy requires intentionality—a decision on the part of two people to become one.

• *Bless your children.* Leaders with children have one primary responsibility toward them, beyond the inherent tasks of protection and provision: children need our blessing. Blessed children (as we discussed in Chapter One) are affirmed in who they are and believe themselves to be hopeful promises of positive contributors to the world. They come to this belief because they have been instilled with a respect for God, their parents, and other people. Blessed children have been challenged to accept responsibility and coached in their development. Parents who bless their children prepare them to be a blessing to others. They do not cripple their children's capacity to be fully formed in their spiritual lives. Instead, they nurture the emotional and spiritual maturation that frees them to enjoy abundant life. These children, by the way, are then free to bless the parents—to confer a sense of well-being that comes from knowing the parents have made the world a better place through their family.

Unfortunately, too many children of spiritual leaders share the sense that they have been unintentionally neglected. It doesn't have to be this way. If you have kids, make a decision that they are not a distraction on the way to your saving the world. They are entrusted to you as part of that world. Connect to them. Belong to them. Don't miss them in the rush to gain the whole spiritual world.

Spiritual leaders who are comfortable in their own home at home feel especially connected. They love to practice belonging with their loved ones.

## Belonging to Friends

You can't choose the members of your family, but you can choose your friends. The unfortunate reality is that too many spiritual leaders ignore this sphere of community. Although they are often surrounded by people, no one in the crowd really is their friend.

Even God wants friends. Three times in the Bible Abraham is called a friend of God (2 Chronicles 20:7; Isaiah 41:8; James 2:23). This friendship overcame some huge obstacles. Abraham could have bailed out over delayed promises and strange requests involving sacrifices. God could have given up on Abraham over making unauthorized trips to Egypt and accepting favors from handmaidens. Their friendship stands as a testimony to their mutual commitment to their personal relationship.

During his last night with his disciples, Jesus said to them, "I no longer call you servants. . . . Instead, I have called you friends . . ." (John 15:15, NIV). This declaration was preceded by Jesus' commitment to them: "Greater love has no one than this, that he lay down his life for his friends" (John 15:13, NIV). Within hours Jesus would back up these tender words with his sacrifice.

If God and the Son of God need friends, so do human spiritual leaders. For leaders, the decision to belong to other people requires decision and determination. Some impediments to friendship have to be recognized and dealt with. The leader must intentionally build specific qualities of friendship into his or her own life.

### Some Impediments to Friendship

Friendships do not develop without having to overcome some obstacles.

*Too Little Time.*   Time is always a precious commodity for leaders. Many existing friendships go undernourished or die for lack of attention because we don't have time for them. Many relationships never get established for the same reason, even when we identify people we would like to get to know better. We simply can't fit them into our already overcrowded schedule. Studies of spiritual leaders note that those who consistently work more than fifty hours per week frequently suffer relational deficits with families and friends, or both.

*Too Little Energy.*   Along with a lack of time comes a lack of emotional margin. Wearied and exhausted by the press of leadership responsibilities, we often do not have the energy to devote to developing or nurturing friendships. The need to experience belonging with some friends is another item to add to a long list of reasons leaders need to guard their boundaries and manage their calendar to guard against overcommitment.

*Misperceptions and Preconceptions.*   Many friendships never get off the ground because of one or the other's preconceptions about the other. Often these opinions have been formed from a distance or from other people's impressions. More friendships could flourish if we moved beyond caricatures or second-hand information and pushed to get to know people for ourselves. A group of pastors who joined together to work for community transformation discovered that many of their colleagues were very different people from the grapevine descriptions of them. As these spiritual leaders worked side-by-side, many became friends.

*Fear of Risk.*   Friendships make demands. Some people fear being too vulnerable to others by becoming friends with them. One church staff leader told me that her senior pastor instructed her not to become friends with any member of the congregation. He told her that being friends would be too dangerous because people might misuse the friendship. Some leaders are afraid that people might find out their shortcomings and failures. This unwillingness to risk makes the leader's role in leading a faith "community" paradoxical, even hypocritical.

Each of the obstacles described confronts leaders with some tough decisions about cultivating friendships. Leaders must set aside time and dedicate energies to creating friends. Leaders must pick their own friends, even if they don't fit the mold or if they surprise some people. And leaders must choose to risk. There are no shortcuts. Friendship is exacting. But loneliness is more so.

## A Checklist of Friendship Qualities

Sometimes leaders find it easier to bond with an audience or a ministry constituency than with individuals in a heart-to-heart friendship. The following checklist of interpersonal qualities provides us with essential characteristics we must possess and demonstrate in order to form genuine friendships.

*Integrity.* Integrity is a character quality that permeates every area of a person's life, including the capacity for friendship. It means promises are backed up, confidences are kept, and people are treated with respect.

*Vulnerability.* Friendships do not develop without some degree of risk. Friends have to demonstrate a certain amount of vulnerability to connect at the heart level. This vulnerability is voluntary, offered from one person to another. Spiritual leaders who work in a culture that punishes vulnerability (perfectionist cultures or environments that have unrealistic expectations) can suffer devastating damage to their hearts.

*Humility.* Some leaders cannot have friends because they are in competition with everyone else. Humility, on the other hand, allows leaders to accept that they are less talented than someone else in some areas. Humility is the opposite of self-centeredness.

Humility can give another soul some attention without demanding reciprocity. The capacity for humility begins with a coming to peace with oneself. A restless spirit or a leader who feels insignificant or inferior can rarely muster genuine humility.

*Willingness to Listen.*  Leaders are used to being heard. Great leaders know how to listen. The act of listening is a gift to a friend. It takes time to hear what someone is revealing about her heart, not just what she is saying with her lips. Active listening requires a commitment of emotional, physical, and spiritual energy. It is the single most important activity that promotes and stimulates growth in the relationship.

*Sensitivity and Responsiveness.*  The many demands placed on leaders can put the squeeze on this essential component of friendship. Friends respond to friends with sensitivity in ways that are appropriate to the situation, that take into account the personalities involved, and that acknowledge the level of accountability and caring that the relationship can sustain. Friends know when to help and how to help. Responding to friends requires that we sometimes put other things and people aside in order to be available and helpful to the friend in need.

*Realistic Expectations.*  Many friendships fail to mature because of unrealistic expectations on the part of one or both parties. Friends will at some point fail us. Can we forgive them? Can others' shortcomings be overlooked for the sake of friendship? Are we willing to extend grace to others? Leaders with a landscape littered with broken relationships probably suffer from unrealistic expectations of others.

## Decisions That Are Friendly to Friendships

The decision to pursue active, growing friendships will require some decisions. You must accept the following conditions in order to cultivate friendships. The first is that you must be willing to be

inconvenienced by investments of time and energy in your friendships, probably by reducing other commitments and, on occasion,
cramping how you would rather spend these precious resources. Your
schedule will probably be altered. Your values may be challenged.

You must decide to pay the price to sustain friendships.
Although this decision relates closely to the first, this is where the
rubber meets the road. Friendships will not develop without the
expenditure of time, priorities, even ministry efforts. Friendships are
reserved for those who count the cost, then pay it.

You have to take a chance. Love without risk is impossible.
Without taking a chance with others you can never know the possibilities for friendships. To take this risk you will have to come face-
to-face with the most terrifying creature in the universe—you!

## Belonging to Coworkers

Great leaders build great teams. Moses had Joshua, Aaron, and
Miriam. David had Abner, his men of valor, and Nathan the
prophet; Paul had Silas, Timothy, Luke, and a bunch of others; Jesus
had the Twelve. One reason these leaders were supported by great
teams centers on the special dynamic between leader and coworkers. The leader belonged to them. The team knew that the leader
saw them as his first line of ministry constituency. The leader shared
his own life with them. Great spiritual leaders still do all three.

### Investing in Your Coworkers

How do you invest in people who work with you? The first way is
financially. If they work for you, take care of them as best you can.
Perhaps you have worked for people who championed your financial needs and others who didn't. Who generated the greatest loyalty? Which one convinced you they believed in you?

Although it might seem redundant to say that spiritual leaders
should invest spiritually in coworkers, my experience suggests otherwise. "We never pray in staff meetings," one disillusioned staff

member told me. For this person, invited from the congregation to join the staff, the move to leadership felt like a bad move spiritually. Those who work around you need spiritual leadership from you. They need to know what you are learning about God and from God. They need to feel their spiritual growth is your primary concern. This is not saying that you are responsible for the spiritual growth of the coworker but that you are responsible for nurturing the spiritual component of the team culture.

Spiritual leadership is stressful. Stress makes high demands on emotional reserves. Smart leaders know that they must invest in their teams by providing emotional support. When asked about how he was doing and how he could be supported, a new team member responded, "I just wish you would call every once in a while just to see how I'm doing." The plea reflected the need and hunger for emotional support. "We don't need to talk about anything in particular," he went on. "It just helps me to keep in touch." That is a fair request for people to make of their leaders.

This emotional support might look different, depending on generational cultures. Younger leaders frequently lament that their "boomer" supervisors do "drive-by" relationships. "I wish my pastor would get to know *me*; just hang out with me sometime," a young student minister once told me. When he heard of this, the lead pastor responded incredulously, "I meet with him every week to check with him on his work." He missed the point! For younger generations it's all about authenticity and relationships first. For boomers it's about getting the job done first, then using any leftover energy for relationship building.

The lesson here is that the way emotional support gets delivered needs to be defined by the recipient, not by the leader. If it doesn't feel like support to the team member, it doesn't come across as support. That is why it is important to ask what the expectations are and learn to speak the coworker's "support language."

In addition to emotional support, leaders signal their investment strategies for their coworkers by ensuring their continuing development. This involves training them in core skills, providing learning opportunities, helping team players identify and develop their strengths, providing people with adequate resources to do their jobs, allowing them to risk, giving them new assignments, and debriefing their ministry experiences and job performances. "I want people to feel they are better off for having worked here," one leader of a denominational organization said. She backed up her intentions by putting developmental money in the budget, placing developmental events and days on the calendar, and documenting expectations for continuing development in the employee-performance agreements of her team. Her actions meant that she put lots of dollars in continuing education, provided workshops for staff as part of the work calendar, and tooled work responsibilities around people's talents in the specific duties of their work assignments, even allowing people to reshape their positions to fit them better.

"Pastor your board," I once told a pastor, as we finished a two-day board retreat where some issues emerged regarding the direction of the church and his ministry. It became clear to me as an observer-facilitator that the pastor lacked personal connection with his board—a situation that was impeding the progress of something that everyone actually wanted to see happen. The lack of pastoral care was complicating the situation, threatening to derail the whole process of redirecting the congregation's expression of its mission.

To his credit the pastor heeded the advice. He began scheduling private meetings with board members, either one-on-one or one-on-two every month. In addition he developed a series of board meeting openings that were designed to ladle care on the members, from special prayer times to teaching times. He conducted another series of phone calls to interface with board members in their spiritual and family development. The result? In just a few months the trust level rose dramatically. The pastor's line of credit was significantly extended. The congregation benefited from a more secure and aggressive board, leading them into the future.

The fellow coworkers who serve on the leader's leadership team are the first line of ministry constituents. Leaders who belong to their team attend to their needs. Incredible as it may sound, we have developed a church culture in North America that often ignores this basic dynamic. Unfortunately, many leaders view their own staff as functionaries. The attention and energy is all about task. Some leaders even resist ministering to their staff for fear that this will compromise their ability to "make the hard decisions" later (when they fire them).

The real result of this approach is a series of broken bodies and souls stretched behind the leader who has used them up, burned them out, and then thrown them away. This sad development has disqualified many spiritual leaders from greatness. Far from leaving people blessed, these leaders diminish other people's lives, as well as their own. For fear of increased vulnerability, they reap the reward of being answerable to the charge that they simply didn't care.

Obviously, the previous paragraph describes a worst-case scenario. Often what happens doesn't approach this extreme. The leader, through spiritual neglect of his fellow leaders, creates a culture that is not nurturing and draining. People become disillusioned as they move into a leadership role, only to find out this cuts them off from receiving ministry care. Some give up leadership and go back into the congregation but go back with a loss of trust and enthusiasm about the leader and his mission.

Those who misunderstand this basic tenet of spiritual leadership erode their own leadership. On the other hand, leaders who get this point build teams of exceptional capacity and loyalty. People love to follow leaders who care for them.

Closely related to the tendency not to minister to staffs is the way leaders sometimes create unnecessary distance from them. "I made a decision years ago not to form close personal relationships with people on my staff," a ministry organization executive admitted to me. As he unpacked his reasoning, he explained that this decision enabled him to escape the charge of playing favorites and allowed him to hold people accountable for their job performance. He had decided to be respected (something every leader would choose). Unfortunately, he thought this came at the price of not belonging to the people with whom he worked. Even though he did all the right things by way of contacting people in crises and of being available to talk with people on his staff, his aloofness and detachment were felt by everyone who worked there.

Aloofness creates a limbic system in the organization that is undernourished emotionally. Limbic connections are the ways that people are connected to each other at an emotional level. For instance, laughter is contagious because it has high transferability along the limbic system of a group of people. If you sit in a theater with two hundred other people, a funny moment in a movie is made funnier by the reaction of the crowd (it's harder to laugh out loud by yourself). Aloof leaders create cold workplaces because their own emotional distance sets the tone for the rest of the organizational culture.

How the leader shares his life with coworkers depends on the leader's personality, work-life rhythms, the nature of the work the team shares, and the personal and family situations of the team members. Leaders have many options for sharing their own lives with coworkers short of establishing a commune and being radically exposed to them (though some have actually chosen this path). Other forms of belonging include sharing social space on occasion or committing to personal life development in a small-group format or taking on a mentoring role. In today's world, opening up one's home and one's heart is still appreciated.

The leader's decision to share his life with his team does not mean that the leader will be everyone's best friend. This is not only impossible; it is undesirable. But the best teams are those who feel a sense of bonding, of sharing life around a shared mission. These teams will charge hell with a water pistol.

## Belonging to Mentors

Mentors are another significant part of the leader's community. These range from life coaches to those who help with ministry and professional development to peer mentors who face similar ministry, life, and learning challenges.

## Life Coaches

I don't know why he took me under his wing, but he did. Bob was an ex-football-coach-turned-high-school-principal who entered my life in my early twenties. His two kids were in the youth group I pastored, so we had a natural mutual interest. We quickly forged a friendship. We fished together, traveled on youth trips together, competed against each other in weight-loss competitions (he cheated), and celebrated their finish by going out to eat together. His house became a favorite hangout for me, then for me and my wife after we married. When we moved two hours away, he overnighted with us about once a month on his business travels. He was a friend, but he was always the Coach, dispensing advice on everything from marriage to furniture purchases to catching bass. I can still hear his signal to get my attention. "McNeal," he always drawled out as a preface to some piece of wisdom he was about to toss my way. I still miss that arresting call, years now after I preached at his funeral.

Bob was unique but he was not alone. Jackie, Earl, Cliff, Ron, are just some others who have played this role in my life. Friends who were and are more than friends. Men whom I could trust had my interest always at heart, even and especially when they challenged me over a decision I made or a leadership direction I took. Men who loved me enough to tell me the truth. Men who were secure enough to let me see them in their own moments of disappointments, setbacks, and vulnerabilities. Men who were and are leaders but who schooled me in more than leadership. They taught me how to live. They helped me become a man.

Sometimes we choose these special people in our lives. Sometimes they choose us. The important thing is to be on the lookout for these "Jethros" in our lives. Jethro helped complete Moses' maturation for life and leadership. All exceptional leaders can point to people who similarly tutored them, especially in their formative years. Leaders who do not have people like this in their lives need to figure out why. It probably is not because candidates were unavailable. The failure lies in the leader somewhere and needs to be researched.

## Professional and Spiritual Mentors

The list of possibilities for this category is as varied as the leader's own background, interests, and learning style. Certainly, great spiritual leaders and teachers of the past and present shape the leader's thoughts. Joining this group are leaders and thinkers from other fields: politics, business, philosophy, military, technology, to name a few. Great leaders tend to be widely read. Part of their capacity for good decision making lies in their curiosity, which in turn fuels their learning and mental facility.

Recently, I met John, a young man in his sixties. His formal education stopped just beyond high school. A late-in-life career change is not the only change in his life. He has also grown past a very narrow worldview (one he inherited from his family-of-origin religious beliefs). All of this came as quite a shock to me. I never would have guessed it, because my introduction to John was over a lunch-time conversation sprinkled with his casual insights on quantum physics, Christian apologetics, medieval mysticism, and political theory. When I asked about his education he simply said, "I borrow from the best minds I can find. I read all the time, at least two books a week." When I asked for his reading list, it was eight pages long! By the way, lest you think he sits in a library or coffee shop all day long, John is a powerful leader—a church planter of a very effective missional congregation.

Whereas the leader is personally intimate with life coaches, such a relationship is not required of these mentors. It may not even be possible. They may have been dead for centuries. The point is, mentors in this category do not have to agree to mentor you. You get to do the choosing.

Choose wisely. These guys get into your head.

## Peer Mentors

Effective leaders all set out intentionally to learn from other leaders who are engaged in similar leadership challenges. Following Jesus' practice with the Twelve, they incorporate into their leadership routine the practice of learning community.

Learning communities debrief the life and ministry experience of the participants. They challenge each other's biases and decisions. They create knowledge together by articulating an expanding awareness of what is going on in their lives, their ministries, and the world around them.

There are several approaches to convening these communities. Some meet in face-to-face sessions of two to three hours once a month, some more and some less frequently. Some communities augment their face time with Internet communication. Some peer-mentoring groups study books together; some retreat together or attend conferences together; others invite resource people to visit their group. My first learning community did all three, including our spouses several times a year. No matter the type of learning stimulus, the major learning curriculum is the same: the participants own the leadership of the learning.

A major component of the leadership development strategy with leaders in my state denomination involves the facilitation of learning communities. We call them learning clusters. One cluster in the state of South Carolina is composed of student ministers. This cluster formed several years ago, initially involving monthly meetings using some of the curricular choices we provide. The cluster has since become much more involved in each others' ministries. These student ministers now collaborate in ministry events, including concerts, summer camps, and mission trips. As good as this is, it's not the best part of the cluster's story. Recently, one of the student ministers told me, "I want to thank you for introducing me to the best friends I have."

He and his colleagues have discovered belonging through peer mentoring.

## Belonging to Followers

Great leaders belong to their followers. This does not mean their followers own them. Nor does it mean they are enmeshed with their followers or that they lack self-differentiation from their ministry community. It means that leaders feel a profound sense of identification with their followers and their well-being and development. Their destinies are inextricably bound together. They are not people who provide resources for the leader's leadership agenda. The leader sees himself or herself as a resource, a servant, to them. The agenda is to improve their lives in some significant way through the leadership agenda.

Biblical leaders demonstrate this kind of belonging. In one of the most interesting encounters of the Old Testament (Exodus 32), Yahweh threatened to annihilate the group of ex-slaves he had just redeemed from Egypt. He complained to Moses about Israel's lack of obedience and revealed his intentions to destroy them. Moses argued back. His willingness to sacrifice himself for his people echoes a theme we run across later in Paul's writings (Romans 9). Jesus, of course, does indeed offer his life in exchange for his followers. Not only for the Twelve. You and I are included in that act of ultimate belonging.

Fortunately, all great leaders are not required to die for their followers. However, great leaders demonstrate a degree of self-sacrifice in order to serve those who follow them. They put the interests of their followers above and ahead of their own. They don't do this on occasion or just during great crises. They do it routinely. It is a way of life. They do not consider this practice heroic; they just accept it as part of the call to spiritual leadership.

At the time of this writing, the world is mourning the passing of Pope John Paul II. The outpouring of love around the world is astonishing to news media pundits and perhaps to many others as well. As they interview person after person about how this beloved spiritual leader affected them and why they feel so connected to him, the consistent reply revolves around a central theme: "He was *for* us. He identified *with* us. He *belonged* to us." One major newspaper ran a summary of John Paul's life under the heading that read, "The People's Pope." The world universally agrees that this Polish priest was a great spiritual leader. Part of that greatness demonstrated itself in the connection he enjoyed with his followers.

———

Great spiritual leaders belong. They belong to their families, their friends, their coworkers, their mentors, and their followers. This belonging provides them with both an anchor and a platform for their leadership. It provides them with both identity and credibility in a sphere of leadership that is ultimately about relationships. They have determined that the benefits of belonging outweigh the risks involved. These leaders have made the courageous decision to be real where it counts the most.

# 7

# THE DISCIPLINE
# OF ALONENESS

We've already acknowledged that leadership is lonely, even if leaders cultivate the kind of belonging we talked about in the last chapter. The truth remains that the experience of leadership is far deeper than loneliness. It involves *aloneness*.

Biblical leaders experienced aloneness. Moses twice trekked to Sinai's rugged heights to be quarantined with God for forty days. He was attended by God alone at his death on Nebo. David knew the loneliness of responsibility as leader of his nation—a loneliness that cannot be ameliorated by an army of advisers. Paul retreated to the desert immediately following his dramatic conversion and subsequent rescue from his enemies. Jesus entered into the prayer garden in Gethsemane alone to wrestle for the salvation of the world. During the heart of redemption's work on the cross, he cried out in desperation from the depths of an unimaginable aloneness, separated from the Father for the first time in the history of the universe.

Leaders who achieve greatness in the spiritual world not only endure aloneness, they build it into their lives. They appreciate the depth of soul making that is possible only in solitude. They even come to the place of craving solitude, not just because a person of their personality type might prefer it but because they find that solitude restores to them the emotional and spiritual center they need for their leadership challenges.

We begin our exploration of this discipline by reviewing the wilderness motif in the formation of spiritual leaders. Our investigation includes both a look at the role of wilderness in forming leaders in the Bible and at how contemporary spiritual leaders can import wilderness into their own lives. In the end, the leader who can practice aloneness is the leader who is comfortable hanging out with God. As we consider how we might foster solitude, we will identify some strategies to help and address key hindrances. Intriguingly, our discussion will bring us full circle back to the leader's self-awareness. We will have arrived where we started.

## The Wilderness Experience

Wyatt leaned forward across the restaurant table, recounting the events of the past four months. A huge project, a year in the making, had flopped at the church he pastors. He was also experiencing marriage difficulties and restlessness among his staff. "I have been wondering whether or not I want to keep doing this," he moaned. Then he added, "I feel like I'm in some sort of wilderness."

"If you are," I said, "you are in for some wonderful discoveries about yourself and about God." Sensing his disappointment that I was not more solicitous, I added, "I wouldn't wish this on you for the world. But I would never take it away from you. There are things you learn only in the wilderness."

## Wilderness Experiences of Biblical Leaders

The scriptures contain many examples of wilderness experiences revealing the developmental role of shaping spiritual leaders. Individuals in both the Old and New Testaments encountered wilderness on the road to greatness. Those experiences highlight different elements of the wilderness motif.

Moses' wilderness is precipitated by his rash attempts to redress his kinsmen's oppression. His forty-year hiatus in the Midianite desert actually culminates in one of the most dramatic of all wilderness experiences. The whole world was changed by Moses' introduction to Yahweh and the subsequent conversations between the two that led to his leadership of the Exodus. Intriguingly, Moses would lead an entire nation through a wilderness experience. Out of that wilderness would come the Ten Commandments and a forged relationship of Yahweh with his people, based on a clearer revelation of who he is and the nature of Israel's mission in the world.

David is driven to the wilderness because of Saul's jealous rage. On the run for his life he discovers the protection of God, the provision of God, and the presence of God. All serve as themes of his psalms. What should have spelled the end of David proved to be his schooling in leadership in adversity. The patience and determination he nurtured during his wilderness sojourn allowed him to emerge from hiding to unite the tribes and to expand and secure the borders of Israel against her enemies.

Elijah defeated the prophets of Baal, only to find himself in danger of being eliminated by Queen Jezebel. His flight and subsequent exhaustion opened him up to a new dimension of appreciation for God's ability to accomplish his agenda. By being humbled, Elijah's leadership increased. By learning God was not limited to only what the prophet could see, Elijah gained the confidence he needed to fulfill his mission and to secure his legacy through recruiting his successor.

Paul's wilderness journey is often considered to be the immediate years in the desert following his conversion. Yet one could argue the wilderness experience for him extended to the decade he spent back in Tarsus following his introduction to the leaders of the Christian movement in Jerusalem. The desert years served to help the young theologian get his head around the revelation of the Messiah on the Damascus road. The apostle had to work through the implications of this encounter for his notions of monotheism and God's mission in the world, the nature of the kingdom, and how God afforded salvation to the world.

The Tarsus years are too little emphasized for Paul's learnings about service and community—hallmarks of his teachings about the church. These years of obscurity are not what one would have predicted for him following his dramatic conversion and his prior stature in Jewish religious circles. Yet Paul's humility in not demanding a leadership role equal to his ability is exactly what qualified him to be the leader of the young movement and legitimized his teachings on how Christians were to relate to each other and to the world.

Jesus seeks the wilderness on his own, tipping us off to its importance in the shaping of spiritual leaders. While others may go inadvertently or even kicking and screaming into the wilderness, the Son of God embraced the sojourn. In the wilderness he crystallized his understanding of the nature of his mission and its personal costs to him. He gained greater confidence in his ability to withstand the enemy of his soul. He emerged with a clear freedom to express himself fully in his divine powers because of his enhanced awareness of his special nature. Jesus' wilderness experience was bracketed by signs of approval from his Father. On the front end it was the voice of blessing and the spirit of power and identity at the baptism. On the back side it was the ministry of angels, serving as recognition of his status in the already, but not yet, kingdom of heaven.

## Wilderness Experiences and Today's Leaders

God still employs wilderness in the formation of spiritual leaders. Wilderness experiences are of life-changing encounters. Leaders travel deeper into self-discovery, typically confronted by new insights about themselves—insights that usually revolve around call or mission, either in terms of clarification or in preparation for some new chapter in the leader's life and work. Wilderness experiences might also revolve around some personal issue or struggle that directly determines the leader's capacity for fulfilling an assignment. Wilderness experiences can yield great rewards for leaders in terms of greater self-awareness, missional clarity, and God-dependence.

Wilderness always involves crisis. It may be precipitated by a crisis, either of the leader's or others' making. It characteristically presents the leader with a decision or set of decisions that must be made. The choices determine the leader's direction at least for the next season of his life. Sometimes the experience of wilderness sets the course of an entire lifetime. It often occurs in key transition times in the leader's ministry.

The wilderness journey can last years or just days. The experience may be marked by intense personal or divine encounter, a more usual occurrence if the wilderness trip is fairly short. On the other hand the wilderness experience might be perceived as excruciatingly trivial and tedious. God may be seemingly absent. In some cases this kind of wilderness does not immediately register on the leader's awareness. It might even be seen only by looking back across the years. In these instances the leader often enters wilderness unaware that it will be preparation for the next stage of life.

It is not a given that leaders grow through wilderness. I see far too frequently that some never see it for what it is. Since most spiritual leaders equate wilderness with a spiritual mountaintop experience, they often fail to accept that unexpected or negative circumstances can be the gateway to the desert. They mistakenly feel that only God can convene wilderness or that they should initiate the experience as part of a planned spiritual excursion. They forget that Moses, David, Elijah, and Paul were chased into the wilderness, hardly of their own accord. When contemporary leaders fail to see wilderness as wilderness, they fail to adopt an appropriate learning stance. Feeling they are in wilderness in error, they scheme to get out or try to reverse their lot, trying to sneak back into Pharaoh's palace. This effort obscures the voice and vision of God. These leaders never turn their faces toward the desert, only their backs.

Another common mistake that causes leaders to miss wilderness learnings is an unwillingness to go it alone. They refuse to take the inward journey, preferring instead to cast about for others' support and insights. They talk to family, to friends, to advisers, to consultants, to other leaders, to supporters in their ministry, to anyone and everyone who will listen. Unfortunately, these many voices can drown out the leader's inner voice or the voice of God—the two most critical voices the leader needs to hear. Certainly, all leaders need input from others to avoid tunnel vision, to check their perspective and information. However, at some point the leader needs to withdraw to reduce the noise. The wilderness is one of those times. Many spiritual leaders stop short of wilderness and settle for far less insight. Truthfully, many leaders, under pressure, go out merely in search of comforting voices, of corroborating voices, of voices that will bolster their wounded egos or bruised spirits. In the wilderness God considers the leader's growth as his paramount concern. This may involve tense discussions and discomfiting insights. Great leaders receive these exchanges as opportunities too precious to give up for fleeting commiseration from well wishers.

Larry met with me often over the course of four years. His marriage was falling apart, his work was suffering, and he had questions about his call to ministry, even questions about whether God cared about him at all. Yet he was determined to grow through the experience. The growth path was painful. His marriage did collapse. He lost his job. He lost most of his possessions. But he lost something else. He lost his self-doubt. He lost his skepticism. He lost his whining. He lost his lack of confidence in God's goodness.

How did Larry attain these wonderful outcomes in the midst of and during a season when everything went from bad to worse? From our beginning conversation it was clear he was searching to discover the lessons he needed to learn. This determination to enter wilderness and stay there until God released him opened Larry up to a new depth of insight into life. He was determined to discover his own contribution to his failed marriage. He accepted responsibility for his lack of job performance, resigning to avoid being pressured to leave. He moved toward God, increasing his prayer life but refusing to "cut God any slack" as he pushed him for answers. Larry is several dimensions better as a person today. His capacity to serve as a leader has exponentially increased. He has been tempered by fire. He is a great piece of heart work.

No leader goes through wilderness unchanged. The transformation may be in the leader's mission or person, or both. Usually, both life and ministry are altered. No leader wants to repeat wilderness. Great leaders, on the other hand, would not exchange the experience for anything. It is often in the wilderness they come to their truest understanding of who they are and what they want to accomplish. In the end they find themselves grateful that God would grace them so profoundly.

## Ways to Import Wilderness

Great spiritual leaders learn to borrow or import wilderness into their lives. They aren't crazy or masochistic. They don't enjoy wilderness, especially the extended or intense kind that usually comes with little warning. However, understanding that practicing aloneness is critical to their soul development and leadership, they proactively seek some dimension of wilderness in their lives. They create opportunities to be alone with God. They embrace silence and solitude. They develop an appetite for the soul nourishment God serves only in private dining experiences.

Importing wilderness will involve one or more key practices.

### Observing Sabbath

God instituted Sabbath to give people rest, which involves more dimensions than just physical relief. In biblical terms the day is designed to disrupt life's usual routines to allow people the opportunity to remember and to reflect. We do well to remember that our lives are being lived against the backdrop of eternity, that we are created by God to enjoy him. Given this remembrance we can then reflect on the status of our lives. Are we living the life we want? Increased self-awareness and missional clarity, remember, are gifts of wilderness experiences. These dimensions of the leader can be addressed routinely through the practice of Sabbath. Absent the practice of Sabbath in our lives, we wind up captured by the temporal, immediate concerns. We lose our way, our perspective, and our center. We forget who we are and why we are here. The loss of Sabbath is one of the major failings of contemporary church life in North America. We are substituting frenetic activity for genuine spiritual vitality.

The practice of Sabbath does not have to conform to a day-long, once-a-week schedule (it might involve half a day, twice a month, or some other routine), nor does it need to follow some prescribed regimen. When I began practicing Sabbath as a pastor, I scheduled an afternoon early in the week. No two weeks of Sabbath experience were the same. The only constant element was prayer, but I mixed it in with reading, with writing, with some exercise or creation, even sleep! Occasionally, Cathy (my wife) joined me for part or all of the time. I pursued Sabbath in my backyard, my study, my bedroom, and in the park near my home.

Two images can help us understand the role of Sabbath and its potential contribution to our lives. The first is that of reviewing game film with a coach. Sabbath affords us the chance to think back over our lives—the events and interfaces with people—to gain God's perspectives and insights. This requires that we develop the capacity to listen for the voice of God among all the voices that clamor for our attention. In this practice of Sabbath we debrief our decisions, our attitudes, our relationships, our leadership, our goals, our achievements, and our challenges. This is a key reflection exercise for spiritual leaders who want to see their life and leadership from God's vantage point. It also enables us to see God, to connect the dots of his activity that we often miss at the time it happens.

I remember once replaying the tapes of the previous week only to discover that the speed bumps I had hit in pursuit of a project turned out to be people! That was not exactly a stellar leadership moment. On other occasions, however, I received kudos from Coach about some great execution of leadership in my personal life, as well as in my role as congregational leader. Coach enjoys celebrating wins!

A second image of Sabbath is one of a marriage date with God, which helps us remember who we are and focuses on our relationship with God. People in growing marriages continue to date just as they did before they got married. Courtship dating helps people explore each other's interests and personalities by spending intentional times of fun and sharing through activity ranging from romantic encounters to quiet conversations to recreational activity to just hanging out together, enjoying each other's company.

This is exactly what a marriage date with God—that great Lover of our souls—is supposed to help us do. He yearns to have fun with us, just hang out with us, to enjoy intimacy with us. He wants to hear our heart, even as he wants to share his heart with us. One of the reasons Jesus was distressed with the Pharisees centered on the way they had subverted Sabbath by turning it into activity, into an obligation, into a burden for people and away from a refreshing encounter with God designed to further intimacy with him. Jesus said Sabbath was intended as a gift for us. Use Sabbath however you need to as a strategy to debrief life and to enjoy God.

## Having Extended Prayer Times

Occasionally, leaders want more extensive interface with God because of a decision that needs to be made or some special personal need. It can also be precipitated by a crisis that pushes the leader toward God. The need for this extended prayer excursion may result from the leader's own realization that his spiritual life needs to undergo some special attention in refurbishment or even renewal. Or it may simply arise from a desire to spend some extended time with the Lover of his soul.

> Jack announced to his staff that he was going to take a personal prayer retreat day at a friend's lake house. For months he had felt restless in his spirit, sensing that he was nearing some watershed threshold in his life and ministry but not knowing much else. He concluded that God was wooing him to a special meeting. Jack packed his Bible, some snacks, a pen, and a journal and headed off to the lake. He spent most of the morning praising God and most of the afternoon mapping out options for the next phase of his life, struggling to hear the voice of God for direction. Toward

the end of the afternoon Jack got a discernable word from the Lord. "I'm up to something" was the entire message. This was not what Jack expected. He had hoped for more definition. Yet he experienced an overwhelming sense of peace and relief upon hearing that simple comment from God (often a signal that the voice we hear is his).

Jack returned from the lake lighter in his spirit and confident in his future. The next few months witnessed a dramatic turn of events and circumstances that redirected Jack into the ministry he is now engaged in. Jack could not have known any of those developments or even have understood them if he had been more aware of them. Jack looks back on that day at the lake as a mini-wilderness, a compressed encounter with God that helped him through a time of personal and leadership transition.

## Fasting

Appropriately practiced, fasting can incorporate components of wilderness into a leader's spiritual experience. Fasting can be done for the wrong reasons, as a religious exercise designed to impress God or others. This was the Pharisees' abuse of this spiritual discipline. They fasted as a way of calling attention to themselves. I once received an e-mail from a pastor who requested I pray for him as he entered into a season of fasting. He told me he was fasting as a way of asking God for some specific things he wanted to see happen in his ministry. Using fasting as leverage on God hardly seems appropriate. It seems far more authentic to enter the time as a way of aligning ourselves with God's desires for us, not the other way around. Every effort should also be made not to broadcast the fasting to others as a way to resist calling attention to ourselves or trying to impress others with our spirituality.

Fasting, whether for a day or for a more extended time, can be a powerful way to focus the leader on God or on some prayer concerns. Its deprivation and discomfort remind leaders that their hope and their provision are in the Lord.

## Journaling

Recording your thoughts requires a leader to engage in reflection and analysis, and to take an inward journey of discovery. Journaling, whether episodic or routine, imports a part of wilderness into the leader's spiritual disciplines. Leaders whose cognitive patterns are more internal, as well as those whose personalities are more reflective, find journaling much easier than those leaders who decide what they think in conversations with others. For the more external types, journaling can have an added advantage of forcing the leader to do some hard introspection, helping to develop a more contemplative side by providing something to do in silence and solitude.

All of these elements of wilderness are part of the leader's continued quest to remain available to God and in constant review of life and leadership. Great spiritual leaders draw essential confidence and spiritual strength from the deep sense of connection they feel with God. Silence and solitude, adopted as regular practices in the leader's life, nurture this connectivity.

## Enemies of Aloneness

Practicing aloneness in today's North American culture requires considered intentionality. Three enemies of this discipline conspire against leaders' need and determination to build solitude into their lives: (1) mismanagement of time, (2) boundaries, and (3) distractions. The most obvious culprit of lost opportunity for solitude is the leader's own mismanagement. This hindrance is the most benign of the three obstacles and is the most treatable. However, without attention, the result of the loss is the same in terms of the leader's soul deficit.

## Time

Every leader battles the issue of time management, but it's especially difficult for those in the ministry, since other people and their needs are notorious for not conforming to our convenience. Nevertheless, great leaders get a handle on this, not only for effectiveness in fulfilling their responsibilities but also in disengaging for soul nurture through aloneness. There is no silver bullet or formula to help the leader here. It requires an act of the will and an unswerving commitment to put solitude on the calendar and protect it. It can help to fix the idea in your mind that time for solitude is part (even a priority) of your ministry assignment and must be scheduled and observed. If the leader considers this time a luxury or something to engage in after other responsibilities are discharged, the leader will not set aside enough alone time. There are simply too many other demands that will always clamor for your time. The smart leader figures out the rhythms of time demands and schedules solitude appropriately. This prudent approach limits the conflicts that would further tempt you to ignore this critical interface with God.

Pastor Charlie took a proactive approach to time management through his appointment calendar. He discovered that scheduling himself away from the office in early mornings provided him, not just sacred space but sacred time as well. It's harder to be interrupted when you aren't around! This is surely why Jesus often left the disciples and went off alone to pray.

## Boundaries

As we discussed in Chapter Two, boundaries serve as the psychological fences that signal to us where our territory ends and the rest of the world picks up. Some leaders struggle with leaving their gates open or allow their downed fences to go unrepaired. In many cases the leader has never conducted a property-line survey to determine where the fence should go or, in worse cases, never put a fence up to begin with. Appropriate boundaries enable leaders to exercise ownership and control over their lives.

Struggles with boundary issues frequently reveal a lack of self-care. Focusing exclusively on taking care of everyone else leads to not taking care of your own physical and emotional health. You don't have time for exercise and rest, let alone for soul-nurturing solitude. Inappropriate voices sometimes tell the leader that self-care is selfish, that only service to others counts spiritually. This stinkin' thinkin' must eventually be addressed and corrected if the leader ever hopes to conquer boundary problems.

Often the leader who recognizes issues in this area will seek help from counselors or others who can help identify the source of boundary violations. Internal rescripting often requires a coach and external accountability to make the necessary adjustments. Behavioral shifts will have to precede emotional shifts in this transformation, because the emotions have been shaped by dysfunction, often from the leader's family of origin.

If you find you have trouble saying no to other people's demands, even unreasonable ones, you need help. If you find you need to be in control, check out your boundary issues. If, under pressure, you retreat from people and refuse help from others, that too is a boundary issue. Your boundaries are too high and too rigid. You need to evaluate your inappropriate boundary issue of shutting people out.

## Distractions

As if ministry demands aren't enough, there are always the distractions—the cell phone, e-mail, the beeper, the television, the Internet, travels, the coffee shop—the list goes on and on. Life can be, and often is, squandered in ten-minute increments. What makes this so insidious is its hidden nature. These distractions siphon off the leader's time and energy like a slow leak in a balloon. Eventually, the leader has to rob time from more strategic pursuits in order to pay back the time and energy deficit created by yielding to distractions. This payback includes time earmarked for practicing the discipline of aloneness.

Great leaders defend against distraction. They have identified their particular vulnerabilities, both in terms of what they find most distracting and when they are most at risk of being distracted. The enemy of spiritual leaders often employs even good things (in and of themselves) as distractions and thereby dulls the leader's effectiveness by thwarting the intentional pursuit of his mission. Chief target of these soul-eroding distractions is the leader's observance of aloneness. Smart leaders turn off devices, retreat to solitary spaces, or do whatever it takes to dial down the background noise of life so they can hear themselves and hear the voice of God.

## A Wrong View of God

Sandy, a woman in her mid-twenties, relayed her spiritual crisis to the conference leader. She had been in a promising relationship for seven months with Brett, but recently he had broken it off, citing some things about Sandy he found he could not live with. The next day Sandy's mom got the news that she had advanced ovarian cancer with a prognosis of less than six months to live. When the conference leader assured Sandy of her prayers, Sandy shot back, "What's the use of praying about this? Brett's gone, and Mom is going to die. It's not as if prayer is going to change any of this."

Too many spiritual leaders, unfortunately, suffer from a wrong view of God that hinders their desire to spend time with him. In Sandy's case subsequent conversation revealed that she held a view of God in which she believed she would be rewarded on the basis of how she measured up. This meant that when things were going great, God must be pleased with her. When things went south, like her dating relationship breakup and her mom's illness, she figured God must be unhappy with her. The real reluctance for Sandy to approach God was her wrong assumption. It did not stem from a lack of belief in God or her lack of confidence in the power of prayer. She just didn't want to face God when he was obviously displeased with her. Not until Sandy's view of God changes will she ever want to hang out with him. There is simply too much fear involved.

Jim's God was the Divine Enforcer. Growing up in a strict and legalistic religious environment, the seminary student had been taught that God had to be obeyed for a person to experience his love and forgiveness. From his youth Jim had worked hard to follow God's law and to do God's will. He had kept himself pure morally and sexually. He had been a shining star in the church youth group. Then as a college student he had been very fervent in evangelizing the guys in his dorm. He had played by the rules and kept his nose clean. Yet he had no sense of relationship with God.

For Jim God represented more a set of demands than the possibility of a meaningful relationship. Not until his second year of seminary did circumstances conspire to lead Jim to experience grace. When he did it overwhelmed him. "Now I get it," he sobbed as he told a teacher what had happened. "I have been in jail all my life, trying to pay for my sin. I never realized what it means to be guilt-free until now." As long as it was about the rules for Jim, a relationship with God was not going to blossom. After all, who wants to hang out with the traffic cop if you're speeding all the time?

Simon was hired as the summer intern in a student ministry in a suburban church. His major responsibility involved teaching in a mid-week student worship experience. After two months a student lay leader asked to have lunch with him. "Why do you think God doesn't like young people?" the leader asked. The question startled Simon. "Why do you ask that?" he inquired. "Because of your teaching," the leader explained. "Your entire emphasis to date has been to inform these kids of what God is against, how their hard hearts are irritating him, and how they need to straighten up and fly right. You've not spoken once of God's compassion, that he is for us, not against us, or highlighted any positive things the students need to put into their lives— like service to neighbors or sensitivity to people who are hurting. It's all been about what the kids should be getting rid of."

Sad to say, Simon didn't get it. Even worse, students in that ministry received a load of bad stuff that summer, delivered to them with religious "conviction." The cleanup will take years, if it is ever finished. Unfortunately, the fallout from having a wrong view of God is not limited to the leader.

Great spiritual leaders are great because they reflect the heart of God to his people. They know God for who he is. They have been captured by him. They enjoy him. Because they do, they hang out with him. And they encourage others to do the same.

## An Unattractive Self

Some people do not enjoy their own company. The idea of hanging out with themselves holds little appeal. They don't find themselves very attractive, which can be a problem when it comes spending time in solitude and silence, the point of which is the inward journey into the soul. Leaders with this problem avoid aloneness whenever possible, even when they are alone.

Pastor Stan rarely comes to the office. He handles almost everything about his ministry with a cell phone and e-mail, not because of a travel schedule but because he likes avoiding other people. At the same time he hates being by himself, so he is always on the phone talking to somebody, anybody. Staff members field a steady stream of e-mails that tie up a large part of every day dealing with their cyberboss. Stan has built a ministry organization that thrives on a frenetic pace of activity. Reflection and contemplation are little valued. Spirituality is monodimensional; only outward expressions count. Stan is missing the boat on greatness. His ministry approach requires a constant influx of fresh people that he can burn out.

Stan hired an executive coach to help him lead his organization to the "next level." The coach perceived that Stan's leadership was being negatively affected by his lack of attention to interior space. When the coach probed the reasons for Stan's style of ministry management, he discovered a leader unsure of himself, carrying huge self-esteem issues. All Stan's activity is a way to drown out voices of recrimination that go all the way back to his family of origin. Stan has himself picked up the childhood refrain, not really believing he is qualified to be in leadership. However, he is too frightened to admit it because this would confirm his worst doubts about himself. He copes by mentally and physically exhausting himself so he doesn't have to deal with his feelings. He isolates himself to keep others from making the discovery about him he is sure they will make if they really get to know him: that he doesn't measure up.

The coach ultimately challenged Stan with two questions: (1) Why would people not like you if they really knew you? and (2) Why are you unwilling to experience grace?

If you find yourself struggling with the same issues that confronted Stan, you might ask yourself the same two questions. The answer to the first question will force you to detail your deficiencies and the standards you're using to measure yourself. Then, instead of some nebulous feeling of unworthiness, you can deal with specific issues. Surprisingly, naming the nemesis is often the first step toward healing.

The answer to the second question gets at the heart of what every leader must learn in order to grow. Properly practiced, the discipline of aloneness is an exercise in grace. Leaders experience grace both from God and from themselves that allows them to deal with failures. Successes are celebrated with grace and gratitude. Leaders who refuse to experience grace never open themselves up for spiritual surgery and reconstruction. And those who have never experienced grace simply don't grace others.

Ultimately, the key for a leader's overcoming a sense of unattractiveness is the journey of self-discovery. Family-of-origin issues need to be explored, along with formative life experiences. Leaders' grasp of their own talent and call also enter this discussion, along with ferreting out their view of God. This is another reason why practicing the discipline of self-awareness is so critical in a spiritual leader's growth and factors into the possibilities for greatness.

Employing the discipline of aloneness allows the spiritual leader to disengage from the world, but not to escape it. In fact, aloneness becomes a key strategy in great leaders for their ability to have an impact on the world. Moses emerged from the wilderness to lead Exodus. David returned from the wilderness to become king. Paul ended his wilderness by launching his missionary journeys. On the cross, in the most profound aloneness the world has ever known, Jesus worked the salvation of the world.

---

The world is waiting for you to walk onto the stage of leadership. It is hoping for a great performance. You will have rehearsed your lines when no one else was looking.

# CONCLUSION
## Choosing Greatness

Great spiritual leaders bless people. Depending on their sphere of influence, this blessing may extend to those in their organization, their spiritual tribe, a region, an entire nation, the whole human race—whoever populates their leadership constellation. Great spiritual leaders are not just given to great issues; they are given to people. In the end, this capacity to bless is the deciding category that elevates them to greatness in spiritual leadership. The spiritual enterprise is about enhancing peoples' lives. God is in the people business.

Leaders who achieve greatness are not only blessings; they feel blessed. They count themselves blessed by those they lead and serve. They are blessed by their colleagues. They are blessed by their leadership team. They are blessed by their friends. They often enjoy the blessing of family. Most of all, they feel blessed by God.

These leaders are marked by gratitude. They consider leadership a privilege. Not unaware of its burdens, they are grateful for their assignment. Even though the price of their greatness may and often does include emotional, physical, and spiritual stress, they count themselves fortunate to have the opportunity to partner with God in his redemptive mission in the world. Though the road to greatness exacts even their lives, they would not swap the journey for any lesser pursuits. They cannot imagine, in the end, doing anything else.

Leaders who practice greatness are grateful to be alive in the world they occupy. They do not shrink from the challenges of their day; they only pine for and work toward a better world. Those who are touched by them think these leaders transcend their circumstances. The truth is, they are completely given to their world. Because they are fully engaged, these leaders serve as portals through which the kingdom of God pours in from the future to invade the present.

Great leaders make countless decisions to arrive at their destination. Tempted in every common point, they resist distraction, overcome demoralization, and discount discouragement as their final option. Instead, they choose determination, optimism, and intentionality. They demonstrate what it means to live courageously in the face of their fears, doubts, and shortcomings.

Leaders who choose greatness are at home with themselves and with God. They are not untouched by the dark side. They do not ignore it; in fact, they are keenly aware of their susceptibilities and vulnerabilities to failure. They refuse to be captured by it or to allow it to be the book on them.

In the end, great spiritual leaders argue for life. They argue for it by their example and by their actions on behalf of others. They wage war on the forces that keep them and others from enjoying the life God intends. Abundant life for them is not elusive; it is the prize they intend to enjoy and to share with others.

We do not know how many leaders opt out of greatness. But we are grateful for every one who chooses it. Because each time a leader makes this choice, the world is better for it. We are better for it.

You are faced with the option of greatness as a spiritual leader. You can choose, as countless others have done, to settle for less. If you do, you die a premature death. And you rob others of the chance to live a better life. If you decide to go for greatness, it will cost you everything you have and are. You will have to surrender your life. You will no longer belong to your personal dreams and petty agendas. Your days and years will belong to the One who believes in you so much he has risked his agenda on you. You will die first, only to discover this is the way to life.

The choice is momentous. Amazingly, it is yours to make.

Choose greatness!

# Notes

1. Cloud, H., and Townsend, S. *Boundaries*. Grand Rapids, Mich.: Zondervan, 1992.

2. McIntosh, G., and Rima, S. *Overcoming the Dark Side of Leadership*. Grand Rapids, Mich.: Baker Books, 1997.

3. Dotlich, D., and Cairo, P. *Why CEOs Fail*. San Francisco: Jossey-Bass, 2003.

4. Goleman, D., Boyatzis, R., and McKee, A. *Primal Leadership*. Boston: Harvard Business School Press, 2002.

5. Buckingham, M., and Clifton, D. O. *Now, Discover Your Strengths*. New York: Free Press, 2001.

6. These questions are treated at length in Reggie McNeal's *The Present Future: Six Tough Questions for the Church*, San Francisco: Jossey-Bass, 2003.

7. For an expanded treatment of the role of community in these biblical leader's lives, see Reggie McNeal's *A Work of Heart: Understanding How God Shapes Spiritual Leaders*, San Francisco: Jossey-Bass, 2000.

# About the Author

**Dr. Reggie McNeal** is the director of leadership development at the South Carolina Baptist Convention. His past experience includes twenty years in local church leadership, ten years in various staff roles, and ten years as a founding pastor of a new church. Reggie has lectured or served as adjunct faculty for multiple seminaries, including Southwestern Baptist (Ft. Worth, TX), Golden Gate Baptist (San Francisco, CA), Fuller Theological (Pasadena, CA), Trinity Divinity School (Deerfield, IL), and Columbia International (Columbia, SC). In addition, Reggie has served as a consultant to local church, denomination, and para-church leadership teams, as well as seminar developer and presenter for thousands of church leaders across North America. He has served as a resource for the United States Army Chief of Chaplains Office, Air Force chaplains, and the Air Force Education and Training Command. Reggie's work also extends to the business sector, including The Gallup Organization.

Reggie has contributed to numerous denominational publications and church leadership journals, including *Leadership* and *Net Results*. His books include *Revolution in Leadership* (Abingdon Press, 1998), *A Work of Heart: Understanding How God Shapes Spiritual Leaders* (Jossey-Bass, 2000), and *The Present Future* (Jossey-Bass, 2003).

Reggie's education includes a B.A. degree from the University of South Carolina and the M.Div. and Ph.D. degrees, both from Southwestern Baptist Theological Seminary.

Reggie and his wife Cathy have two daughters, Jessica and Susanna, and make their home in Columbia, South Carolina.

# Index

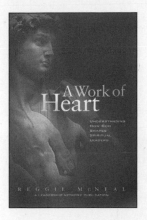

**A WORK OF HEART**
*Understanding How God Shapes*
*Spiritual Leaders*
Reggie McNeal
Cloth
ISBN: 0-7879-4288-X

"It is not just the skills of ministry that are important. The heart-sculpting work of God creates
quality ministries. *A Work of Heart* explains how
God is shaping each of us for future service."

—Bob Buford, founding chairman, Leadership Network

"We've read leadership manuals ad nauseum. We've attended every high-
powered conference imaginable. We've bought the T-shirts, the three-ring
binders, and all the right soundbites. But if we're honest, we're in serious drift
mode, and we know it. . . . In *A Work of Heart*, Reggie McNeal has given us
nothing less than CPR for the leader's soul, a book that moves us beyond
leadership "how-tos" to the lifeline of genuine influence—our own intricate,
passionate journey with God."

—Sally Morgenthaler, author, *Worship Evangelism*

"Everyone committed to developing leaders must study Reggie McNeal's
understandings of heart shaping, and in doing so, will experience their own
hearts being sculpted."

—Donald O. Clifton, chairman, The Gallup Organization

Reggie McNeal proposes that effective spiritual leaders must become experts
in matters of the heart—particularly their own. They must learn to discern
God at work in their own lives, shaping their hearts to embrace the particular ministries to which they are called. *A Work of Heart* shows how God pre-
pares leaders today just as he did in biblical times—and how God creates
these leaders in order to share his heart with his people.

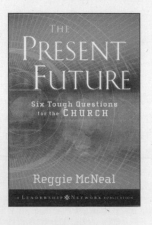

**THE PRESENT FUTURE**
*Six Tough Questions for the Church*
Reggie McNeal
Cloth
ISBN: 0-7879-6568-5

"This is the most courageous book I have ever read on church life. McNeal nails the problem on the head. Be prepared to be turned upside down and shaken loose of all your old notions of what church is and should be in today's world."

> —George Cladis, senior pastor, Westminster Presbyterian Church, Oklahoma City, and author, *Leading the Team-Based Church*

"With humor and rare honesty Reggie McNeal challenges church leaders to take authentic Christianity back into the real world. He's asking the right questions to help us get back on track."

> —Tommy Coomes, contemporary Christian music pioneer and record producer, artist with Franklin Graham Ministries

"Reggie McNeal throws a lifeline to church leaders who are struggling with consumer-oriented congregations wanting church for themselves. *The Present Future* will recharge your passion."

> —Rev. Robert R. Cushman, senior pastor, Princeton Alliance Church, Plainsboro, New Jersey

In this provocative book, author, consultant, and church leadership developer Reggie McNeal identifies the six most important realities that church leaders must address including recapturing the spirit of Christianity and replacing "church growth" with a wider vision of kingdom growth; developing disciples instead of church members; fostering the rise of a new apostolic leadership; focusing on spiritual formation rather than church programs; and shifting from prediction and planning to preparation for the challenges of an uncertain world. McNeal contends that by changing the questions church leaders ask themselves about their congregations and their plans, they can frame the core issues and approach the future with new eyes, new purpose, and new ideas.

## THE PRESENT FUTURE DVD SET

Reggie McNeal
DVD
ISBN: 0-7879-8673-9

In this 4-DVD set, Reggie McNeal personally presents the ground-breaking ideas and insights in his best-selling book, *The Present Future*.

Filmed live before a studio audience, these DVDs show Reggie at his most appealing and compelling best. His blend of humor, personal story, and challenging approach has captivated thousands of people. Package includes leader's guide and participant's guide to facilitate use of the DVD with church groups and leaders.

As in the book, in the Present Future DVDs McNeal takes up the challenges of leadership for the church—what must leaders do in order to move beyond "churchianity" to Christianity, to move from church growth to kingdom growth, to develop followers of Jesus rather than just church members, to shift from planning and programs to new ways of moving into a missional future.

By changing the questions church leaders are asking themselves about their congregation and their plans for the future, McNeal seeks to frame the issues so that the future can be approached with new eyes, new purpose, and new ideas.

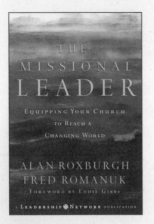

NEW!
**THE MISSIONAL LEADER**
*Equipping Your Church to Reach
a Changing World*
Alan Roxburgh and Fred Romanuk
Foreword by Eddie Gibbs
Cloth
ISBN: 0-7879-8325-X

"Discontinuous change wreaks havoc among congregations and pastors who aren't familiar with the new terrain. When it comes to navigating this new land, Roxburgh and Romanuk have my ear and gratitude. Effective, dependable, useful . . . their wisdom is helping retool our congregation for daring and robust witness. And among my students—who feel change deep in their bones, both its threats and opportunities—this book is a vital companion as they begin their ministries."

— Chris William Erdman, senior pastor, University Presbyterian
  Church; adjunct faculty, MB Biblical Seminary Biblical Seminary

In *The Missional Leader,* consultants Alan Roxburgh and Fred Romanuk give church and denominational leaders, pastors, and clergy a clear model for leading the change necessary to create and foster a missional church focused outward to spread the message of the Gospel into the surrounding community. *The Missional Leader* emphasizes principles rather than institutional forms, shows readers how to move away from "church as usual," and demonstrates what capacities, environments, and mindsets are required to lead a missional church.

Experts in the field of missional leadership, Roxburgh and Romanuk outline a strategic change model that can be implemented to help transform a congregation and its leaders. They also present the factors that define the character of an effective missional leader and show how a pastor and other clergy can lead their congregation to best serve their church and larger community.

Alan Roxburgh is a pastor, teacher, writer, and consultant with more than thirty years' experience in church leadership, consulting, and seminary education. He works with the Allelon Missional Leadership Network in the formation of leaders for the missional church.

Fred Romanuk is an organizational psychologist who has led strategic planning initiatives for many large organizations in Canada and the United States. He has also worked with senior executives in assessing and developing the capabilities of people in leadership roles.

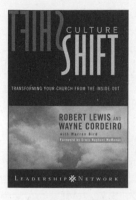

**CULTURE SHIFT**
*Transforming Your Church from the Inside Out*
Robert Lewis and Wayne Cordeiro,
    with Warren Bird
Foreword by Erwin Raphael McManus
Cloth
ISBN: 0-7879-7530-3

"Like snowflakes and fingerprints, every church's culture is unique. Learning the art of cultural analysis and cultural formation shown in *Culture Shift* is indispensable for church leaders."

— John Ortberg, teaching pastor, Menlo Park Presbyterian Church;
author, *If You Want to Walk on Water, You've Got to Get out of the Boat*,
and *The Life You've Always Wanted*

"If you are looking for a quick fix, don't buy this book. But if you're looking for the secret to a faithful, thriving church, then buy out the store."

— Bill Easum, president, Bandy & Associates; author, *Leadership on the Other Side*

*Culture Shift,* written for church leaders, ministers, pastors, ministry teams, and lay leaders, leads you through the process of identifying your church's distinctive culture, gives you practical tools to change it from the inside-out, and provides steps to keep your new culture aligned with your church's mission. Real transformation is not about working harder at what you're already doing or even copying another church's approach but about changing church culture at a foundational level.

The good news is that you already have everything you need—but you must look within for radical, transformational power. Your job is to develop a healthy atmosphere and let the Holy Spirit do the work through you. Once this fundamental shift has occurred and the new habits and values become central to everything your church does, a healthy, energetic, God-honoring church will be unleashed into a world that is desperately crying out for it.

Robert Lewis is pastor at large of Fellowship Bible Church, a nondenominational church in Little Rock, Arkansas. He is also the chairman of the board of Fellowship Associates, a church consulting and leadership training organization.

Wayne Cordeiro is senior pastor of New Hope Christian Fellowship O'ahu in Honolulu, Hawaii. He is also the founder of Pacific Rim Bible College, an institution that trains, develops, and supports emerging leaders.

Warren Bird is an ordained minister on staff at a church in metro New York City. He is the winner of a Gold Medallion Award for religious publishing.

**LEADING FROM THE
SECOND CHAIR**
*Serving Your Church, Fulfilling Your Role, and
Realizing Your Dreams*
Mike Bonem and Roger Patterson
Foreword by Greg L. Hawkins
Cloth
ISBN: 0-7879-7739-X

"Somebody said the hardest instrument to play is second fiddle. But since Jesus had one or two things to say about serving and submitting, this is a rich field. Mike Bonem and Roger Patterson have addressed a key need with wisdom and clarity."

— John Ortberg, author, *If You Want to Walk on Water, Get out of the Boat*; teaching pastor, Menlo Park Presbyterian Church

*Leading from the Second Chair* offers an invaluable resource to leaders who serve in second (and third and fourth) chair roles, enabling them to become more productive, proactive, and fulfilled. The book reveals the paradoxes of second chair leadership. These leaders must be subordinate to the top leader yet lead in their own right. They should be deep in their expertise but wide in perspective. And they must be content in their jobs yet remain enthusiastic about their dreams for the future.

Mike Bonem and Roger Patterson share their own and others' experiences of failure and success in this vital role. They offer support and practical advice for reshaping the way second chair leaders can serve well and improve the overall performance of their church or organization.

Mike Bonem has been a consultant to churches, judicatories, and businesses for more than twenty years. His company, Kingdom Transformation Partners, offers coaching and leadership development for first and second chair leaders.

Roger Patterson is the associate pastor of West University Baptist Church in Houston, Texas, where he has served for eight years. He is a second chair leader who loves to invest in the development of other leaders for the expansion of God's Kingdom.